MW00440996

ICONS

Also by Dodie Kazanjian

Alex: The Life of Alexander Liberman
with Calvin Tomkins

ICONS

the absolutes of style

DODIE KAZANJIAN

ST. MARTIN'S PRESS
NEW YORK

The pieces "The Chanel Suit," "The Image Consultant," "The Wedding Gown," "Victoria's Secret," "Manolo's Mules," "The Winter Coat," "Diamonds," "The Armani Jacket," "The Boot," "Thin Thighs," "Hemlines," and "The Little Black Dress" were first published in *Vogue* magazine. Courtesy *Vogue*. Copyright © 1989, 1990, 1991, 1992, 1993, 1994 by The Condé Nast Publications Inc.

"The Kelly Bag" first appeared in *The New York Times*.

Art Direction by CHARLES RUE WOODS AND JAYE ZIMET

Design by IRENE VANDERVOORT

Library of Congress Cataloging-in-Publication Data

Kazanjian, Dodie
Icons / Dodie Kazanjian.
p. cm.
ISBN 0-312-13518-1
1. Fashion—United States—History—20th century. 2. Costume—United States—History— 20th century. 3. Dress accessories—United States—History—20th century. I. Title.
TT507.K352 1995
391'.2'097309045—dc20 95-21645
CIP

First Edition: October 1995
10 9 8 7 6 5 4 3 2 1

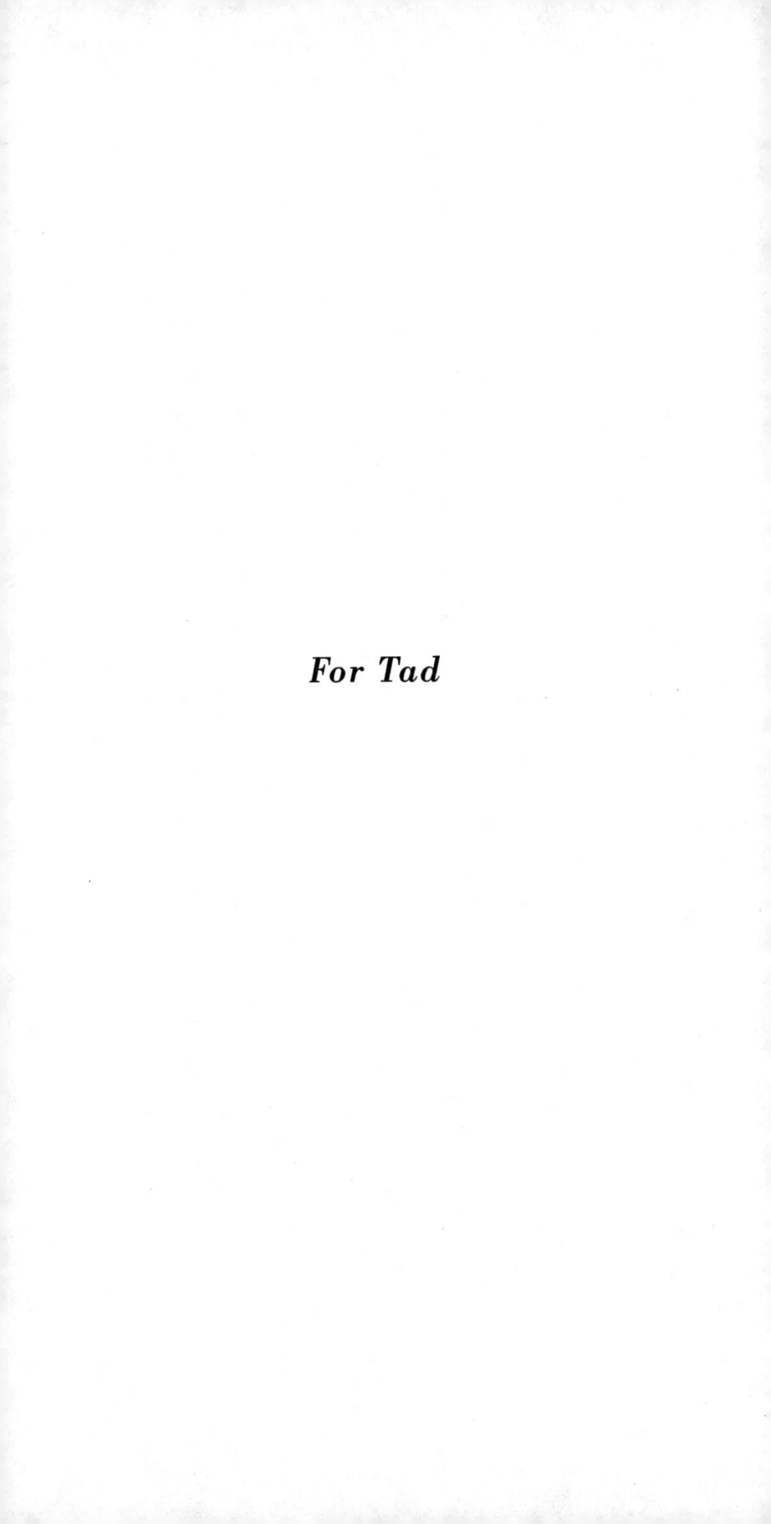

For Tad

contents

illustrations

Front Jacket: *Manolo Blahnik*

The Chanel Suit: *Karl Lagerfeld*

The Kelly Bag: *Alan Dingman*

The Wedding Gown: *Vera Wang*

Victoria's Secret: *Steven Broadway*

Manolo's Mules: *Manolo Blahnik*

Pearls: *Verdura*

Diamonds: *Verdura*

The Armani Jacket: *Giorgio Armani*

The Boot: *Manolo Blahnik*

Hemlines: *Norma Kamali*

The Little Black Dress: *Isaac Mizrahi*

Back Jacket: *Karl Lagerfeld*

acknowledgments

My thanks to all the designers, consultants, and fashion insiders who appear in this book. I am hugely grateful to Manolo Blahnik, Isaac Mizrahi, Norma Kamali, Vera Wang, Karl Lagerfeld, Giorgio Armani, Steven Broadway, and Alan Dingman for doing the original drawings that enliven my pages; thanks also to Ward Landrigan for making available the drawings of Verdura. Sally Richardson, Charles Rue Woods, Jennifer Weis, Tina Lee, and Irene Vandervoort of St. Martin's Press, and Andrew Wylie, my agent and friend, are responsible for turning these pages into a book. (Any errors, as Christopher Buckley taught me to say, are naturally theirs.) And my special thanks to Anna Wintour, *Vogue*'s brilliant editor and an icon's icon, for her encouragement and support.

introduction

At fifteen, I yearned to be a fashion model. Unfortunately, my body wouldn't go along—instead of growing tall and willowy, it stayed short and (hateful word) petite. Then I wanted to be a fashion designer, but the only clothes I ever designed were my own. Although the allure of high fashion persisted, I never felt that it was really for me; like many women, I tended to dismiss the whole notion of couture as irrelevant, trivial, overpriced, and somewhat silly. But way in the back of my mind was a memory of myself as a toddler, wearing a white angora bonnet with an angora strap under the chin. I loved it so much that I kept it on indoors and out. It made me feel wonderful, glamorous, beloved. It was an icon of sorts, and as full of buried meanings as Proust's madeleine.

In 1989, I became a writer for *Vogue* magazine. Not a fashion writer—my main beat was contemporary art and artists—but now and then I was told to go out and report on some aspect of fashion that interested me. I felt a little like an anthropologist taking notes on some exotic tribe. But what fun it turned out to be! Here I was, a fashion outsider, tooling along the inside track. For the first time, I could shop without feeling intimidated or guilty. And what I went looking for, it gradually dawned on me, were the icons of our time, the stuff that makes us feel wonderful, glamorous, and beloved.

Along the way, I got to meet a lot of high-powered men and women who are fashion icons themselves—Manolo Blahnik, Karl Lagerfeld, Norma Kamali, Donna Karan, Bill Blass, Isaac Mizrahi, Vera Wang, and others. A more exotic bunch would be hard to find, but one thing I learned is that they don't all belong to the same tribe. Very few of them even agree about what fashion is, or where it's heading. "I can't stand fashion," Isaac Mizrahi told me. "Who needs fashion today? Fashion is totally out." But like my little white angora helmet, the lure of it just won't go away.

the Chanel Suit

I've never had a Chanel suit. A Chanel suit is something my mother wore, and I always thought I wasn't old enough, or grown up enough, or tall enough to have one. But I always thought I'd have one when I was in my thirties, which is where I am now. It's one of those big events in a woman's life, like getting married or having a child. I got married last year for the first time. We're discussing the child. And I find myself thinking more and more about a Chanel suit.

Anyway, I finally decided to dare it.

It's eight o'clock on Thursday morning, February 15, and I'm getting dressed to go shopping at Chanel. What should I wear? My four-year-old blue YSL coatdress is the ticket—it's authoritative, it has a name, and it's not my usual black.

I arrive at five minutes of ten, five minutes before they open. The big glass doors are not locked, to my surprise, so I walk in. They're vacuuming inside. One of the women in the Chanel salesgirl's uniform—black Chanel sweater and skirt, white blouse, ropes of pearls, and beeper—invites me to sit on the sofa while they take the last few moments to primp the store for its open ing. At ten on the dot, "Can I help you?" asks the same Chanelmaiden. She is friendly and casual, an Italian girl from the Bronx who puts me immediately at ease.

"Yes, please. I've never worn Chanel, and I'd like to try."

Going upstairs is part of the Chanel ritual. A stairway has drama, and Coco always had one at her famous rue Cambon shop in Paris. This one is Coco–New York. It's not a bit old-world. It has glitz, with vertical strips of cut mirror to your left as you ascend. At the top of the stairs, I ask if I've come at the wrong time of year—between seasons or something like that. "It happens you've come just at the right time. My name is Patricia," she says, giving me her hand.

Does she mean the right time, literally, because it's that rare moment when I'm the only shopper in the store? No, she means that the spring/summer collection was shown in Paris last week, and the new line has just started to arrive. She points to a rack of clothing set into the far mirrored wall. I ask about a white Chanel suit with a long fitted jacket I had seen in a magazine last summer. Is it still available? "Forget that suit," she says, authoritatively. "Just forget it. That was last year's." She walks me over to the suit rack and shows me a couple of little suits—one is a vanilla yellow color with a raglan sleeve, and the other is navy.

"Okay, I'll try these on."

"No-no-no," she says. "I don't have any in

your size. These are all size 40s and 42s." The line has just started to come in, she explains. Then she walks me over to a countertop, asks me if I've seen the collection, and shoves a huge black binder in front of me before I can answer. On the left-hand page, there's a Polaroid of a model wearing a suit with a very short skirt; on the right, there's an entry for each size, with space after it for the names of customers who have placed orders. If the size is highlighted in yellow, it means it's in stock. Patricia asks if I'd like to see the collection on video. "Sit over here," she says, planting me on a brown suede settee and offering coffee or orange juice. The video theme song, "Better Than Ever," fills up the audio space. "We're better than we've ever been before. . . ." Models sashay across the screen in Chanels that don't look like the ones my mother wore. Thanks to Karl Lagerfeld, these are tighter, with thigh-high skirts and brighter colors. I'm a little worried that now I may be too old for Chanel.

Fifteen minutes later, as the video is winding down and the theme song is beginning to get on my nerves, people have begun to block my vision of the screen. There are more Japanese than you see bidding on paintings at Sotheby's or Christie's. Patricia comes over and asks me what I like. "There's a little white V-necked bouclé jacket that seems to go with everything that . . ." Before I can finish my sentence, she's sitting next to me with the book on her lap opened to the page with the little white jacket that's shown with everything from a chiffon evening dress to a bikini.

"Forget that jacket. That's the jacket of the season. You'll never get it. And besides, the press has made a big deal about it, and there's an unbelievable waiting list. See?"

Waiting lists for Chanel suits? I know I'm on Fifty-seventh Street, but I thought that was art gallery lingo. "What do you mean, waiting list?" She shows me. On the right-hand page, there are hundreds of names—names in tiny print cramped in after each size.

"How many people will get this jacket?" I ask.

"Oh, one in each size, perhaps, sometimes two. But no promises." (This little jacket isn't cheap. It's $1,665.)

All right. Let's give it another try. I tell her I like the light yellow–beige suit with white piping and relaxed-looking shoulders. She opens the book to just the right page, and we study the line for size 34. There is no yellow horizontal line, which means the suit hasn't arrived from Paris yet, but the line is already full of names. She manages to squeeze mine in and puts a *9* next to it. I'm number nine in line for this one, behind two Japanese names. Her beeper beeps, calling her to the telephone. All over New York, women are paging Patricia for Chanel suits. What chance have I got?

"What else did you like?" she wants to know.

"Well, there was a wonderful beige suit that reminded me of the one I liked last summer—the jacket is long and fitted and the model had her sleeves pushed up." Patricia finds it in the black binder. For this one, she writes my name in with a *6* next to it; the same two Japanese names are in front of me. My heart sinks. Maybe I'm not Chanel material. I've never flown to Marrakesh for the weekend with a grand duke, or been presented at court. Patricia senses my anxiety.

"While you were watching the video, I was able to pry some suits away from other salespeople for you to try on. You can't buy them, because they're reserved for other people, but at least you can see how they fit."

The dressing room is ample, not threatening, with fawn Ultrasuede walls, a settee and one chair, a countertop, and a three-way mirror. We start with a cropped fuchsia jacket and a chiffon skirt. The chiffon skirt is the latest style for evening, she informs me. I'm after a suit for daytime, but what is interesting is that a Chanel 34 fits me perfectly. Next, she shows me a black bouclé suit with a jewel neckline, gold buttons, and the matronly look I always associated with Chanel when I was a child.

"This is a 34?"

She assures me it is. When I get into it, sure enough, the jacket is boxy, not fitted, and I feel it's wearing me. She agrees. (There's no such thing as high pressure at Chanel.) But the skirt is a great fit. "Leave the skirt on and try on this little white jacket," she suggests. As I'm doing so, there's a knock on the door. It's my thirty-something friend Lucy, English and pregnant, who like me has never worn Chanel but feels it's about time. She likes the little white jacket, which I can't buy because umpteen people are already waiting for it. Patricia brings in two more suits—both navy. No go on either. The top pockets on the long jacket hit at just the wrong spot—exaggerating me where I don't want to be exaggerated. The tunic is too overpowering. Out they go, and back she comes with a black cotton suit loaded down with gold buttons. Lucy shakes her head no as I snap the big gold belt buckle shut. "I still like the white jacket best on you," she says, heaving herself out of the settee to go to her eleven o'clock appointment. Thanks, Lucy. She tells Patricia she'll be back in May after she delivers.

After trying on a few more suits I can't buy, I ask Patricia, "Now what?" We sit on the settee with the black binder. She recommends that I get on the waiting list for a suit that she doesn't have but that she is sure will be "the suit of the season," a pastel yellow bouclé with a silk satin bow at the neck. "It's a tiny suit. Not everyone can wear it," she says. "But you can." I'm number four on the list for this one, but she notices that nobody has reserved it in pastel blue in size 36, so she puts me down for a 36, too.

"I hate to buy clothes that are too big and need lots of alterations," I protest.

"Trust me. We have a great seamstress."

Flipping through the black binder one last time, she spots "a classic little suit" like the white jacket, she says, that comes in black or white, and nobody has reserved the black in my size. I'm number one for this one. Hooray!

It's twelve fifteen and I'm late for an appointment. Patricia tells me that a shipment may already have arrived, and I should check with her in the morning to see if any of my selections have come in. "It could take a week or three weeks," she says. She takes my telephone number and I ask for her last name. "Oh, everybody calls me Fish," she says with a laugh, pushing a card in my hand. Her name is Patricia Pesce.

"I'm going away for a week," I say. She looks anxious and takes the number where I'll be. "I'll call you there," she says. "But you have to be ready."

The next morning at ten I call Patricia. I ask what the procedure is if something does arrive while I'm out of town. "There's a three-day grace period given to everybody," she says. "I'll worry about it when it happens. I'll do some juggling, but let's not worry till the time comes." She's reassuring but seems in a hurry to get off the phone.

The week passes. Should I call? Meanwhile, I notice that hot little white jacket in the Sunday *Times* magazine. Also, a long fitted black jacket that looks like bouclé, over a chiffon skirt.

It's ten thirty Monday morning, a week and a half after my visit to Chanel. When I call and ask for Patricia, I'm told she's at lunch. She's what? I hang up. At twelve fifteen, Patricia calls me back. "Nothing has come in yet," she tells me right off. "But did you see *it* on the cover of *Vogue?*" See what? (Of course I didn't. I only write for *Vogue*. I'm the last to see it.) "Our suit. Remember I told you it would be the suit of the season?"

I'm a little out of focus but then catch on. "Oh, yeah. The little one with the satin bow at the neck."

"Yes. Yes."

"Oh, now I'll never get it, now that the press has a hold of it—and the cover of *Vogue*."

"Not everyone can wear it," she says, just as she did before, bucking up my spirits. "And besides, you're already number four for this one."

Would it make sense for me to try to get it at another Chanel boutique? "No," she assures me. "I'm doing everything for you. I'm not permitted to fax until it gets into the stores."

Fax? What does faxing have to do with this?

She explains that once a particular suit arrives, she can then fax Beverly Hills or one of the other Chanel boutiques for it—like putting out an all-points bulletin.

February 28, 10:40 A.M.: my phone rings. "This is Patricia from Chanel. I've got my hands on a chiffon skirt."

"Chiffon? But I wasn't waiting for chiffon."

"I thought you might like to have a little separate."

"I don't think so. What I really want is a suit. You won't forget me?"

"Of course not. I'll call you the minute something comes in."

March 3, 10:30 A.M.: the phone rings. "I got the black suit in," says a now familiar voice, excited this time.

"Great. I'll try to get in this afternoon."

"Fine. I'll hold it for you."

Patricia has become my protector at Chanel. I change my plans and go that afternoon. I arrive at two fifteen. Since it's a Saturday, the place is jammed, and hopping. After about five minutes, I find Patricia. She goes into a back room and returns with my suit bagged in plastic. Lifting the plastic very carefully and slowly, she says, "Isn't it beautiful?" Before I can answer, she tells me that it's going to take a few minutes for a dressing room to free up. "Make yourself comfortable."

Time passes. I hear the insistent sound track of the video starting up again: "It's better than ever, we're better than ever. . . ." It's now 2:55, and I've been waiting forty minutes for a dressing room. Patricia notices me looking at my watch and rushes over. "It'll only be another five minutes." A couple of minutes later, she signals to me that a room is becoming free. "Wait a minute while I get the suit." As she goes to get the suit, another salesperson starts to claim the dressing room. "That's mine," Patricia says very clearly. She tells me to come on in. As soon as I try on the black suit, which I never even had the chance to see before getting on the waiting list, I know it's not for me. It doesn't have that young Lagerfeld look. It's more of a Chanel from the past. But do I dare let it go? It may be the only chance I'll have. All I can afford is one suit. Patricia senses my dilemma. "You can let me know on Monday morning."

March 5, 10:20 A.M.: I call Patricia and tell her that the black suit isn't what I want. "All right," she says. "I'll call you when one of your others comes in."

Time is passing and I'm wondering whether I'll ever get a Chanel suit. Not only is *my* Chanel on the cover of March *Vogue*, but I just received the April *Vanity Fair* today, and Madonna is on the cover wearing a white chiffon Chanel dress. It's true that you see much more of Madonna than of her Chanel, but at least she's got one.

March 14: I call Patricia. "Nothing's come in yet."

March 15: One month since I first went to Chanel.

March 16: I call Patricia from out of town, a touch of desperation in my voice. "Nothing yet, dear," she says.

March 26: I call at 1:30. Patricia can't come to the phone; "She's with a customer." Patricia calls me back at 5:40. "Nothing yet." She pauses, then adds, "One of the suits *is* here, but we're number four for it." My mind does some quick arithmetic. That means I could wait nine more days before I can even try it on. "That's all I can say at this point. We have to wait for the three in front of us."

"But I'm going away for a week on Sunday."

"Call me on Friday."

"Is it time to start faxing?" I ask.

"Not yet. But think positive."

March 28: There's a message on my machine—"This is Patricia from Chanel. Please call me. I've got very good news for you."

I call her immediately.

"I've got it for you," she says triumphantly.

"Which one? The little pastel? In yellow?"

"Yes. Yes. Yes. Size thirty-four."

"What happened to the three people in front of me?"

"They're all out of town till next week or the week after." So they've all lost their turns—only three days of grace, you know. Very democratic. "I can't get in till four tomorrow, is that okay?"

"See you tomorrow."

March 29, 4:00 P.M.: Patricia is waiting for me by the cosmetics counter at the door. We climb the stairs and go into the same dressing room. She goes to get the suit. The tension is building. What if I don't like this suit? Once again, I think maybe I'm not meant to have a Chanel in this life. A minute passes, then another. Where is she? Suddenly, I see Patricia at the doorway carrying something covered in plastic. She stops to answer a saleswoman's question. I'm straining my neck to catch a glimpse of the suit, but she's holding it with her right arm, away from the doorway.

Finally, she comes in. She hangs it on a hook, lifts the plastic, and steps back.

It's such a pale yellow bouclé, much paler and softer than I had imagined, like Devonshire cream, and it's piped in the silkiest white satin I've ever seen. The whole thing is lined with silk satin, and the lining is channel-quilted (a straight up-and-down quilting, as opposed to the average cross-hatched kind), just like the old Chanel suits used to be, and the jacket even has a gold chain sewn all around the inside hem, a signature detail Coco invented to make her jackets hang evenly. It has the right Lagerfeld look. As I slip into it, I feel as though I'm becoming a different woman—sophisticated, immaculate, possibly Parisian. Patricia claps her hands. We both know it's a success. "It's gorgeous," she says, smiling and jumping up and down. I can hear the video's music starting up outside—"Better than ever, better than ever, we're better than ever, now."

And so am I.

August 1990

the image consultant

Women who use image consultants don't want to talk about it. It's okay to delegate interior decorating, cooking, and sometimes even child rearing to experts, but the idea of hiring an expert to show you how to dress, style your hair, do makeup, walk, talk, and perhaps even think is taboo. It may be one of the last taboos left in America. I was curious about this reticence, so I decided to hire an image consultant to find out just what it is that nobody wants to talk about.

Also, I have a couple of minor image problems that I could use some help with. I'm five feet two and want to be five feet six, and I've always wished I looked all-American. My grandparents were Armenian, but I am always being taken for a South American.

To find the right image consultant for me, I got a copy of the *Directory of Personal Image Consultants* and called about five or six in New York City. After fifteen minutes on the phone, it was Annie Brumbaugh who impressed me the most.

She came to my apartment for our first meeting. "I will show you the key to the height thing," she said, right off. "It's a matter of proportion." This sounded good to me, better than the psychological claptrap that all small people are used to hearing—like, "you're as tall as you think you are." And then she said, "This hair is like Eastern Europe," about my willful black hair that's nearly halfway down my back. "I'm not dedicated to cutting off all your hair, but with Laurent, I'll show you just what to do." (Laurent Delouya owns La Boîte à Coupe hair salon in New York.)

Brumbaugh, five feet six in flat shoes, with cropped, neat, light brown hair, large giraffe-patterned glasses, and a perfectly proportioned black sheath, was all confidence. A youthful forty-four with energy to spare, Brumbaugh studied fashion design in London before opening her own atelier in Marrakesh, where she was a fashion designer for five years. She moved to New York City and founded Annie Brumbaugh/Wardrobe Works in 1983. "This is the world's most useful dress," said Brumbaugh about her black sheath. "It's like a shell." It was by Gibson Palermo, a pair of designers from San Francisco whom I had never heard of. For the first fifteen minutes, we discussed my lifestyle and I showed her magazine pictures of what I thought I needed—a white cotton Chanel suit and a black-and-white-check dress from Emporio Armani. I also mentioned that I liked Michael Kors's clothes for more casual occasions. Then she said, "Let's get started in your closet."

My closet consists mostly of black and white Saint Laurents with a couple of black and white

Geoffrey Beenes thrown in, and one Valentino dress, the only navy item in my closet. After five hours of uninterrupted work in the closet—pulling nearly everything out (evening clothes not included) and trying it on—Annie decreed all of it out of proportion or out-of-date, except for one black sleeveless lightweight wool dress by Geoffrey Beene. Everything else was either too long or too full, therefore pulling me down in height. After a glance at my costume jewelry—mostly Saint Laurent again, with some Kenneth Jay Lane from the seventies—she declared it all too overpowering for me. She asked to see my makeup. When all I brought out was one soft black eye pencil by Chanel that I use to fill out my less-than-adequate eyebrows and to draw around my eyes, she looked slightly shocked and spoke gently of blushers and lipsticks. Then we talked turkey. Annie's fee would probably come to $2,000. And I had to be willing to spend at least $3,000 on clothes.

For the last ten years, I've had little time for shopping. I've been overextended. I take on too much. Until last year, I lived in Washington, D.C., at the Watergate, which had a handy YSL boutique on the premises. I did most of my shopping by telephone. I'm a person who wants a couple of perfectly cut black suits, two crisp white cotton blouses, and one great black skirt for daytime. I don't want much else. I wondered how I would react to shopping with a stranger.

Exactly two weeks after Annie's visit, we met at the Fiftieth Street entrance of Saks Fifth Avenue. She had spent the day before scouting in the store for what she thought I needed. She whisked me up to The Fifth Avenue Club (headquarters of Saks's personal shopping service), where she had about twenty pieces of black, white, and black-and-white clothing for me to try on. Annie warned me that because it was late in the season (this was the end of May) and because of my difficult size (size two or four, depending on the designer), it was hard to find anything. The good news, she said, was that everything would fit me because the clothes were all petites. Ugh. *Petite* to a small person—at least to this small person—is a dirty word. To me, petite suggests cute, off-the-rack, poor quality, nonstyle; it also makes me feel psychologically shrimplike.

I couldn't bring myself to try on one short-sleeved black jacket made of a silk that had too much shine. So I started with a long white jacket—somewhat the shape of the jacket of the Chanel suit I had shown Annie at my apartment. When I asked about the Chanel suit—which I would have lived in during the summer—she said, "It doesn't exist in your size and it's too expensive." This white jacket was a far cry from Chanel, but it was on sale for $130, and it had a proportion to it that Annie said made me look taller: the long fitted jacket over a short fitted skirt. The idea was a good one, but the quality wasn't there. We continued. Two long-jacketed black suits later, and after two faux-Chanel blouses (both under $100), a black-and-white polka-dot silk pajama pant and top, and an electric purple rayon crepe dress, we came to the only nonpetite piece in the lot: a black linen dress by Ferragamo, something I would never have chosen for myself. Long, halfway down my calf with a fitted torso, and belted. To my surprise, it looked great on. And then a black-and-white-check skirt by Escada—again nothing I would have picked, but it fit me well. We eliminated a few dresses and the shiny jacket and asked for alterations (mostly taking in at the waist) on the rest. The bill came to $2,500, and I still didn't have my white Chanel suit.

It was after two o'clock. We looked at earrings on our way out. Earrings, Annie said, are essential because they draw the eye to the face, thereby adding height. Nothing struck me, however, and I resisted Annie's suggestions. We stopped for a quick lunch, and she pulled out of her black leather Mark Cross bag "the perfect earrings," as she described them, by Gabrielle Sanchez—a pearl on a fine gold wire that goes through the pierced ear. I tried to put them on. No luck. The curved wire was difficult to maneuver through the ear hole. I tried again. It was impossible. She said that I *had* to have them, but that we could put it off until tomorrow. Then over to the Margo Hasen boutique, where Annie had a short black rayon knit dress on hold. It was see-through in places I don't like to be seen through.

Over to Guy Laroche, where Annie had a hot pink cotton suit with black dots on hold. It looked quite good to me, but it still wasn't the Chanel suit I craved. It was a lunch-at-Le Cirque suit, and I don't do lunch at Le Cirque. Couldn't we try Chanel, I pleaded, or Saint Laurent or Valentino? Annie said she had checked with all of the above and none of them had anything for me. Was this Guy Laroche suit for me, or did the hot-pinkness make me look more South American? As I was resisting, I could see that this was irritating my image consultant. Time was passing. I bought it; $1,300, alterations and tax included.

It was nearly six o'clock, and we had quite a few more places to go as we worked our way up Madison Avenue. Next stop: Pilar Rossi, where Annie had the tiniest black linen short-sleeved bolero waiting for me. It fit, but it had shoelace closings on the sleeves that dangled to the elbows. Wouldn't it be better for me without the laces? No, said Annie. A short-short jacket gives you height, and it's a steal at $200.

When we reached Kenzo, they were locking up. It was six thirty, and we decided to call it a day. That night, I couldn't sleep. I was annoyed that I had actually bought all those clothes from Saks that I didn't really like. In the morning, I called Annie and told her about my anxiety. She said we'd talk later.

If you hire an image consultant, be prepared to devote a lot of time to it. The next day at 11:00 A.M., Annie arrived with Stella Moustoukas, the best seamstress I have ever come across. In an hour and a half, Annie and Stella helped me into 75 percent of my summer clothes and rejiggered every one to just the right proportion for me. As they worked, shortening the hemlines, making the skirts narrower, I could see myself growing taller in the mirror.

Annie brought up the Sanchez earrings again, but I said I didn't want to deal with that problem at the moment. I dashed off for an appointment. During the day, Saks delivered some of the clothes, and I tried them on that night. Except for the Ferragamo dress and the Escada skirt, I hated every one. The material was cheap, and the cuts weren't what I was used to. I called Annie and told her they had to go. To my surprise, she agreed and told me that that was one of the advantages of shopping at department stores; they take everything back. The fact that I was being an impossible client didn't seem to faze Annie in the least.

The next day, I met Annie at twelve thirty at Kenzo. I knew Kenzo's work but had never thought of it for me. She had me try on an extravagantly pleated white cotton voile skirt, a more casual version in aqua with big parrots on it, and red pants with a matching jacket that knotted at the waist. No soap. I thought they all played up the ethnic look I was trying to escape. But I spotted some scarves—oversize and made of voile. I bought two of them. As we were leaving, Annie announced that now was the time to try on the earrings, which by this time had become torture items in my mind. Upstairs in the serene dressing room at Kenzo, she was able to put them in, to my surprise, without too much difficulty. They looked better than I expected, but they weren't knockout, and the thought of removing them made me queasy.

My ears wired with the pearls, we walked quickly to Morgenthal-Frederics Opticians, where I was hoping to get the black Ray-Ban sunglasses I've been trying to find time to buy for the past five years. They didn't have Ray-Bans in black, but they did have a designer copy for three times as much. I walked out wearing a yellow tortoise job with a matte finish. Now for feet. Annie wanted me to go to Giordano's, a shoe store on First Avenue that sells only small shoes. But we had no time, because I had a three o'clock appointment. We went to Charles Jourdan instead, where I knew size 4½ existed. Annie tried to get me interested in flat shoes. Major balking on my part. If it's not three inches high, I'm not interested. Time was up, thank God.

We met at a suite in the Dorset Hotel at one o'clock on Monday, where Gibson Palermo, the San Francisco–based designers, were having their trunk show. She ran me through the line—modern classics, priced from $500 for a black cotton sheath to $5,000 for a taffeta ball gown. I spotted the black sheath on a rack. It was the summer version of what Annie had been wearing when I met her, in a cotton "popcorn" fabric. That was what she suggested for me. A muslin of the dress had to be made in order to achieve the perfect fit, and I was told the dress would appear in about six weeks. It cost $512 plus $75 for the muslin, which they keep on file if I order again.

The time had come to tackle my hair. At La Boîte à Coupe, a trendy but pleasantly relaxed salon on East Forty-eighth Street, Laurent Delouya sized me up and said, "This is *really* thick hair. But you can keep it long if you do it right." He explained that all the volume was at the bottom of my hair and was pulling me down. Annie stayed right beside me while he snipped away. "He's taking weight off the ends of your hair," she said. "You want your hair to be light, not just hanging."

Laurent recommended hair combs. "It pulls the whole head up. Gives the illusion of taller. Shows the face. It's very important for you." Annie ran down to a drugstore to buy black combs, which he deftly inserted. When he finished, I loved the result. I still felt like myself, a feeling I've never had after leaving a hairdresser. Annie whipped out four pairs of clip-on earrings by Gabrielle Sanchez, three of which I liked and agreed to buy. On the street, as we parted at six forty-five, Annie said, "You do look taller." When I got home, my husband opened the door and said, "Thank God. I was afraid they were going to tame your hair."

In the morning—only a few things left now—we started at ten o'clock. First stop: Bergdorf's. At the cosmetics department, Annie took me to the Prescriptives counter. I kept telling her I prefer Chanel, but there was a great push to go to Prescriptives. Finally, I insisted that it had to be Chanel.

We had good luck at the Chanel counter because Alan Goldman, a young makeup artist who has his own private clientele, happened to be there. It took him forty-five minutes to work his wonders on me: light foundation, concealer, powder, eye contouring and brow brushing, in addition to rose satin blush and sheer amethyst lipstick—the "no-makeup makeup." The next appointment was with Maria at Renaissance on West Fifty-sixth Street for a facial and pedicure. She was fabulous—expert and gentle.

Annie and I had been going at it pretty intensively for a week. I was still five feet two with unruly dark hair and had spent more than $4,500. But I had learned some things. My own sense of what looks right on me was largely confirmed. It had been a fine-tuning, not a transformation. Annie was sensitive enough to know that she had a tough nut to crack, and she knew when not to push me. As a result, I have quite a few new clothes that fit me better than the old ones, and the old ones now fit better, too. There had been some upsetting moments and some exhilarating ones. Doors had been opened. I now have a great seamstress, and I plan to go back to Maria and Laurent. I won't wear foundation, but I did buy lipstick and blush. And I'm thinking about a flat shoe by Saint Laurent that Annie and I looked at. Laurent even said that he could dye my hair blond. But, of course, that isn't what I really want. Being tall and all-American was always a fantasy of sorts. Annie had dealt tactfully with the reality and made me like it better.

September 1989

the kelly bag

For years and years, I've wanted the Kelly bag. To me, it's not just the supreme symbol of the world's most exclusive status boutique, Hermès, it's the ideal bag to carry. Roomy, stylish, exquisitely made, pickpocket proof with its twin closing straps and padlock—it's the bag for all seasons.

Over the years, though, whenever I got up the nerve to ask about one, the response was the same: As a salesman at Hermès announced to me a year ago, "Good heavens. There's a four-year waiting list." From his expression, it was obvious he thought I couldn't afford one.

But I kept seeing the Kelly bag around town, on the arms of New York's Chosen Ones—Brooke Hayward, Adele Chatfield-Taylor, Betty Bacall. How did they do it? I dreaded another humiliation. I had a vision of the dear old lady who once questioned the price of a brownie at Eli Zabar's E.A.T.; the proprietor snatched the morsel from her trembling fingers and ordered her to "Leave my store!" Hope springs eternal, though; it seemed to me that with a recession on, the Kelly market might have loosened up a bit, and so, last fall, I decided to risk it once again.

The Kelly bag has been called the Kelly bag ever since the mid-1950s, when Grace Kelly was often photographed carrying one. Derived from a much larger piece of luggage, which was used to carry the saddles, bridles, and other riding tack of grand dukes and royals, it began its life as a ladies' handbag in 1930. In recent years, it has proliferated in various sizes, colors, and leathers, at prices ranging from $2,500 for a mini in calf up to $10,000 for the large-sized "croc." For about $30,000, you can get a version with a solid gold, diamond-studded padlock.

Not quite nervy enough to show my face in the Fifty-seventh Street Hermès boutique, I decide on a *coup de téléphone*. "I don't have anything in stock," says a saleslady named Marjorie. "And we're not taking special orders." To my surprise, she sounds genuinely sorry. "What color did you want, though?"

"Black," I say.

"Oh, that's the most difficult to come by. Everybody wants black."

Why, oh why, is this particular handbag so permanently out of reach? Perhaps because it's top-of-the-line Hermès, so well known it doesn't need the big "H" clasp that is on some other Hermès bags. Status, but quiet status. And Hermès itself is *unique au monde*, the three words that J. P. Morgan said were the most expensive he knew.

Five generations of the Hermès family have kept it that way. The business was started in 1837 by Thierry Hermès, just around the corner from its present world headquarters at 24 rue du Faubourg St.-Honoré in Paris. Its wholesale riding harnesses quickly became known as the best available. In 1879, Thierry's son, Émile-Charles, shifted to retail and added saddles and other riding gear. The Hermès saddlery catered to the greatest stables of France, the Imperial Russian Court, and wealthy South Americans. When the automobile unhorsed this market in the 1920s, Hermès shifted gears with great style, branching out into handbags and luggage. Clothing, clocks, watches, jewelry, silverware, gloves, and diaries followed. The famous Hermès hand-printed silk scarf first appeared in 1937.

The firm's worldwide growth in the fifties and sixties assured that the sun would never set on the Hermès empire. It now has more than 250 sales outlets, and its 1990 sales totaled an estimated $460 million. And yet, the Kelly bag is still being made by hand, slowly and lovingly, on the fourth floor of 24 rue du Faubourg St.-Honoré; 9,000 are completed—and signed—each year by twelve skilled workers, who have apprenticed for ten years with a master, in the tradition that goes back to Thierry Hermès.

"Do you think it could take years before I get one?" I ask Marjorie.

"Yes and no."

Rumor has it that you can find a black Kelly bag in the Hong Kong Hermès, but I haven't been to Hong Kong lately. It seems hopeless.

But good heavens! Here I am going to the movies with Brooke Hayward and her beautiful medium-sized black Kelly bag—just what I long for. A little sullenly, I ask her how she got it.

"It's a copy," says Brooke. "I'd never dream of paying that much for a handbag."

A copy? *Bien entendu!* In this age of appropriation, the Kelly bag has been knocked off from Helsinki to Katmandu. Trust Brooke to find the right knockoff.

"I've been getting them for ten years," she says, "at a little store on Fifty-fourth Street."

I go there the next day. Kelly lookalikes on the walls, on the counters, on the floor; also fake Pradas, Célines, Guccis, and a couple of Mark Crosses and Bottega Venetas—all of them looking enough like the originals to fool a master shopper.

I ask for a medium-sized "Kelly" in black calf, and three models are promptly produced. How much? Three hundred and seventy-nine dollars and no waiting. The woman next to me is looking at a black lizard "Kelly" for $900. The store owner, a plump, talkative man in his shirt-sleeves, is merrily playing to the clientele; holding a black "Kelly" against his hip, he says, "I brought this bag to America in 1952, before Grace Kelly ever saw it."

"Do you always have 'Kellys' in stock?" I ask.

"Always—except that this year, for the first time, I've been running out, so sometimes you'll have to wait a month."

These "Kellys" are made in Italy by the same people who make leather goods for Céline, Prada, and other well-known names. The owner of this boutique helped to channel his father's export-import business into handbags in 1950; his children now make this a three-generation concern. Within fifteen minutes, I have bought the last medium black calf "Kelly" he has in house. Three generations of knockoffs will never really match five generations of Hermès, but who's to know? As Julia Child would say, "Remember, you're alone in the kitchen—nobody's watching."

Ah, but I'm watching. I'm the original princess on the pea. So, when Marjorie from Hermès calls me two months later, out of the blue, and asks, "Are you still interested in a black Kelly?" my heart somersaults. I'm there when the store opens the next morning, wearing my pale pink "Napoleon" Hermès scarf. The bag has a softness and a glow to it, a quality beyond quality. It costs $2,800, but, with the right care, it will last thirty years or more. (Brooke admits that she gets a new copy every few years.)

"We just received a shipment of fifteen," Marjorie tells me. "None of the black calves will go out on the floor—some of our clients have been waiting four years." Then how is it that I can buy one? "Some people may have found them at one of our other boutiques. You're just lucky."

I weigh it in my hands, hold it against my hip. The line is unmistakably elegant, inimitable, *unique au monde*. It's large enough to hold my hairbrush, my tape recorder, my Filofax, and my dreams of glory. The seduction is complete.

I won't buy anything else this year. I promise. With my Kelly bag, I won't have to.

August 25, 1991

the wedding gown

It's the best of times. It's the worst of times. It's ecstasy and it's agony intertwined. It's the most personal moment in a woman's life, and also the most public. The wedding day when a bride plays the lead in her very own drama. When she's onstage, acting out every conceivable fantasy, from queen of the universe to sacrificial victim. But the great question is, what will she wear? Anxiety compounded. And what will her mother wear? And her bridesmaids and flower girls and other supporting players?

I got married two years ago, and the subject of the bridal dress was so loaded that I managed to put off thinking about it until ten days before the wedding. I was having lunch with my editor at *Vogue*, and she asked me if I was wearing white. (I'd never been married, but I was in my middle thirties.) For years, my fantasy was to look like Audrey Hepburn in *Funny Face*, wearing Givenchy's tea-length white tulle wedding gown. But that would never do for my eleven-o'clock-in-the-morning, immediate-family-only ceremony at Trinity Church in Newport, followed by an immediate-family-only lunch at the Clambake Club. My editor saw that her question was bringing on an attack of the Bridal Dress Traumas—she knew all about the BDTs, having put off buying her own dress until the day before her wedding. She suggested I go directly to Geoffrey Beene, which I did. I did wear white—a short white piqué with the Hepburn silhouette—and I've been living happily ever after.

But not every bride-to-be has a *Vogue* editor to see her through. At least not until this fall, when Vera Wang opened her Bridal House Ltd. on Madison Avenue. Vera Wang was a *Vogue* editor for seventeen years. A forty-one-year-old woman of Chinese ancestry, with long dark hair and delicate features, she was working as a design director for Ralph Lauren in 1989 when she decided to get married for the first time. She was astonished to find that in spite of all her fashion expertise, the choice of a wedding dress was as traumatic for her as it is for everybody else. She ended up buying three bridal dresses as her wedding scenario went from simple to elaborate and then to even more elaborate. "I felt incredibly insecure about what to wear," she told me when I visited her a couple of days before the opening of her Bridal House. "I really didn't know what was appropriate or what wasn't. When you're talking about a wedding, it's a fine line between fantasy and good taste, even for someone who's a fashion professional. No question."

Wang's own wedding was a brilliant white-tie affair at the Pierre, with four hundred guests, Hank Lane's twenty-two-piece orchestra, and an endless flow of caviar and Cristal champagne.

It was the happiest of occasions and it also gave birth to a blessed event: a brand-new business. Having been struck by how little help she got from department stores in dealing with her own BDTs, she decided to go into the bridal business in a big way, and from a high-fashion point of view.

"I saw a business opportunity," she says. "There isn't another area of fashion that hasn't been covered, re-covered, redesigned, and super-overdeveloped, from Speedo swimwear to Nike shoes to couture to the new couture. Bridal was an outlet for me to express myself, and my own design sense, and my own experience. But it was also a chance to do some very interesting fashion. *Bridal* does not have to be a dirty word."

Fashion insiders say that Vera is becoming the Martha of weddings. What she offers is a tremendous degree of personal service. To help a prospective bride over her BDTs, Vera Wang and her associates offer, on the average, about forty-eight hours of concentrated attention. They focus on her unique physical aspects, on the kind of wedding she has in mind, on the setting, and on the bride's sense of herself as well as her fantasies. It's a total psychological and logistical fix. They will happily provide every detail of her and her attendants' attire, from a headdress ("very important") to bridal slippers. Vera will even run up a $350 custom silk charmeuse garter with an interfaced bow, because each bridal thigh is sui generis, most of the ready-made bridal garters are too wide, she feels, and in any case, one size definitely does not fit all.

The big department stores have their own bridal salons, but they offer nothing resembling Wang's frenzy for personal service and customized detail, and nothing like her selective range. She carries designs by Carolina Herrera, Arnold Scaasi, Pat Kerr, and a raft of European dressmakers, all personally selected by Wang. She has cutting-edge dresses of every description (including a strapless and nearly skirtless number in skin-hugging lace), and she also has more traditional creations by Priscilla of Boston and other well-known names. Vera has her own workroom across the street from the Bridal House, at the Mark Hotel, with two designers, an assistant, and six hand sewers who can match anything that's done at the European couture houses. The key concept here is made-to-order. Although Vera feels the word *couture* is too pretentious for her operation, she is now negotiating deals with Karl Lagerfeld, Giorgio Armani, and Christian Lacroix that will allow her to sell their bridal gowns, which are traditionally the climax of their collections but which are rarely produced. She's working with Donna Karan, Michael Kors, and Rebecca Moses. She's hot on the trail of Ralph Lauren. And she has sewn up the services of Victor Edelstein, designer to the British royals. And Vera, of course, is in there too, designing gowns and altering other designers' prototypes for the very particular needs of her clients.

"Every body is different, and we can dress every one of them," she says. "We have dresses for the woman with terrific breasts, or a terrific back, or terrific arms." Needless to say, she also has dresses for less-than-terrific bodies. She got into designing for mothers of the bride because so many of them seem to be surpassingly interested in how *they* look on the Great Day. (The mother and mother-in-law, of course, are major contributors to the BDTs.) And her ambitions go beyond the wedding—she also has a made-to-order line of late-day and evening dresses for satisfied brides and their retinues, whose patronage she wants to hang on to. But at the moment, the wedding is the main thing—the wedding in its fashion totality, which includes dresses for prenuptial dinners as well as the postnuptial reception, and which extends to bridesmaids, flower girls, ring bearers, and everyone else. She will even advise the groom.

"I see myself as an arbiter of taste," she says.

Vera will style the whole wedding for you if you want her to. "Nobody else was doing that," she found in the course of her own wedding. "Someone should really be styling the wedding. I don't mean just selling dresses, but really, really styling—the veil, the gloves, the slippers, the garter, the costume jewelry for the attendants so that they don't all wear their little knickknacks. So I thought I would take on this challenge."

All this service and applied taste doesn't come cheap. The wedding gowns at Vera Wang's range from $2,000 to $24,000 or more. And the customized accessories, many of which she designs herself, are priced accordingly. She strongly recommends that her clients come to her at least three months before the wedding date if it's going to be a major do. This is about the amount of time it takes to mount a Broadway show. And make no mistake, a Vera Wang wedding is a *coup de théâtre*. "It's theater, no question, absolutely," she says. "Whether it's an afternoon wedding in Greenwich, Connecticut, on the lawn with a tent, or at the Rainbow Room at night, it's the most theatrical moment in a woman's life."

I can relate to that. Last weekend, just before talking with Vera Wang, I went to a wedding on Long Island that was the best piece of theater I've seen since John Guare's *Six Degrees of Separation*. The bride and groom held their reception in a cornfield in Wainscott, under a white tent festooned with cornstalks, where a country and western trio played on and on and the bride danced barefoot in the beige mini that had lurked beneath her long bridal skirt during the ceremony. The dress was by Badgley Mischka, but the wedding was styled by the bride and a couple of friends who had spent eight months planning every bucolic detail.

Vera Wang is aching to do a country wedding, but not in the Hamptons. "I think of really beautiful gardens, or of Newport, by the sea," she says. "And there's a dress that I'm dying to do, which is white cotton piqué. It's one of the freshest and most innocent and classy fabrics that a designer can use. I would love to do something romantic and big and clean, with an incredible sash and bow in back. Maybe the sash would even be a bright color. Kind of *Ryan's Daughter*–feeling."

I ask her what she would do for a Texas bride.

"In Texas, you need a *lot* of detail and a *lot* of romance and a *lot* of stuff. The Texans I know are all fun. They feel no guilt or angst. At any Texas wedding, the girl is going to have to look sexy. They dress for their men. I see some tits, décolleté, off the shoulder. Short in front and lo-o-ong in back. Real theater. I see lots of jewelry and lots of veil and lots of hair. And I see her being totally disheveled by the end of the evening."

What about Los Angeles?

"L.A. brides work out a great deal. They're fit. If you don't have a great body out there, you might as well move out of California. I have skintight dresses that are like bathing suits. I'm going to pull one out for you."

She disappears for two seconds and comes back with something that looks like a long, puckered spaghetti strap. "Here's the L.A. bride. Are we right? It ain't nothing without the body in it. But it's everything with the right kind of body. Stretch silk jersey. Now that's a cutting-edge bride. Nothing under it except a great tan."

The daughter of a Chinese-American businessman, Vera Wang was born in New York City. While she was at Chapin, she was a "serious, serious" figure skater and danced in competitions. She studied art history at Sarah Lawrence and then did graduate work at Columbia. *Vogue* editor Francis Stein spotted her while she was summer-temping at Yves Saint Laurent on Madison Avenue; she went to *Vogue*, and within a year and a half she became one of its youngest editors. Her areas of expertise were accessories and photographic sittings. But even before she embarked on her seventeen years at *Vogue*, Vera had always wanted to be a fashion designer. So when Ralph Lauren asked her to come and design women's accessories and furs for him a couple of years ago, it was a dream come true. But then—ta da!—came marriage and her new career.

The next time I see Vera is at her opening party, on a Thursday night in September. My husband and I squeeze in through the huge crowd that spills onto Madison Avenue. A fantastic mannequin bride fills the show window—her "dress" is entirely composed of richly hued flowers by Pure Madder-lake. Inside, a live model in a Vera Wang–designed white duchesse satin wedding gown with black velvet trim poses on the spectacular circular French limestone staircase. Bobby Short plays the piano at the top of the stairs, and fashionable body types toast one another with champagne and quail eggs stuffed with caviar. Bridal dresses hang discreetly on the walls—no department store excess here; Vera doesn't want her premises to look "all merch" (Vera-ese for merchandise)—along with first-class Bonnards and Van Dongens from the Wang family collection.

Vera, who designed the premises in collaboration with the firm of Stephen Sills and Associates, is in one of the intimate salons in back. She's dressed in black, as usual—one of the latest creations from her made-to-order evening dress line. (She's dying to do an all-black wedding dress, but she hasn't found the client for it.) Next to her is a many-splendored wedding cake, with columns between the layers that echo the stenciled oak columns throughout the store. "The cake is by Sylvia Weinstock," Vera says. "She's one of the world's greatest bakers. She does all the biggest weddings."

I'm wearing my own white piqué knee-length wedding dress with black trim. (I wear it all the time.) "Absolutely wonderful," she says, beaming approval. "No question." What a relief.

The scent of success is in the air. A first-night hit. But will people pay for this sort of thing, with a recession and war clouds on the horizon? "Regardless of what the times are, the wedding is still a sacred right of passage," says Vera. Marriage is recession proof. The sky's the limit, and Vera Wang knows how to get you there. No question.

December 1990

Victoria's secret

What is Victoria's Secret? Every other week, it seems, a new catalog turns up in the mail, chockablock with lush, full-bodied beauties bursting out of peacock and fuchsia push-up bras or reclining languorously in see-through black-lace body stockings. Shafts of sunlight caress soft, slightly moist skin, and tropical foliage and blue water wink through the billowing bedroom curtains. The same faces and figures fill lavish double-page ads in a dozen or more national magazines. Around the country, Victoria's Secret boutiques and Victoria's Secret bath shops are becoming as ubiquitous as McDonald's. There were five hundred at last count, all hyper-romantic boudoirs perfumed with potpourri, purring with classical music, rife with the trappings of femininity.

Victoria's Secret is one of the most successful marketing phenomena of the decade. I order from the catalog when I can get to it before my husband does (I recently learned that he also receives it at the office). I browse in the boutiques. Although some of the merchandise doesn't exactly thrill me—the workmanship is not Parisian, and the underpants don't really fit—I keep ordering more.

Just what is going on here? Let's take a closer look, starting with the catalog. It's a very slick piece of work. One of the firm's executives recently told *Women's Wear Daily* that the catalog was much sexier in the mid-eighties, when men and women were photographed together in various stages of undress, but that's a joke; the photos now bring the *viewer* into the picture, so close that there's no room for anyone but you and the model. Victoria's Secret models are a phenomenon in themselves. (It's becoming fashionable for movie stars and other big-time honchos to go out with them.) They are pretty without being glamorous. More often than not, these houris look you right in the eye, not so much come-hither as here I am, more *Playboy* than *Vogue*.

The Victoria's Secret woman is not a fashion model, nor is she the girl next door. If she's a wife, she's somebody else's wife. But she's more likely a wife-mistress, with her loose, slightly disheveled hair and one shoulder strap falling down. Don't get me wrong. There's nothing cheap about her image. No stiletto-heeled, red-garter-belted cuties in the manner of the old Frederick's of Hollywood, the mail-order lingerie business that's been going since 1946. She's not just a plaything in undies. As a matter of fact, more than half of the catalog is now devoted to showing her in skirts, dresses, sportswear, and other ready-to-wear "outies." Her fingernails are colorless and sensibly clipped, her makeup minimal. I can relate to her. She may not be a Gorilla

Girl, but neither is she a *grande horizontale*.

So, okay, the secret is that she's two (or more) women rolled into one—just like the rest of us. She appeals to me as much as she does to my husband, and often for the same reasons. But why *Victoria's* Secret? The implication here is sexual hypocrisy, isn't it? Straitlaced morality on the surface, unbridled lust behind the scenes. (Queen Victoria's secret, which was not so secret, was an extended dalliance with her Scots gillie at Balmoral.) After three decades of topless dancers and bottomless sexual candor, are we heading back to the double standard?

I certainly feel pangs of Victorian guilt whenever I pass the chain's boutique on Madison Avenue. I'm always tempted to go in, but gosh, the construction workers out front will know just what I'm going in for. Today there are no construction workers, so I sneak inside. The interior is as cozy as a boudoir. The scent is pervasive and a little cloying. Soft classical music floats from hidden speakers. (You can buy the tapes or the CDs at the counter, along with books of love poetry, all specially packaged.) Panties, bras, camisoles, lace bustiers, and satin teddies crowd in on me from all sides, whispering enticements. Body lotions, perfumes, and bath foams compete for counter space.

"May I help you?" murmurs the pretty saleswoman.

I ask her about a "whisper-light baby doll" that I had seen in the catalog.

"Oh," she says, "we're entirely separate from the catalog. We don't carry the same items."

I wander up a flight of stairs past an enormous oil painting of a female nude, all soft pastels, nothing to disturb a Victorian sensibility like mine.

There are a few customers, one of them male. A saleswoman is freshening a satin peignoir with a hand-operated mister. After combing through way too many displays of underpants—I can always use some white underpants—I finally find one that is not a thong, a bright floral print, or a wisp of lace, and take it to the dressing room. As you might imagine, the tiny room is pink, with a triple looking glass framed in Victorian gilt. Reflected in it, the underpants seem voluminous on me in the rear. Is the callipygian look coming back? Bustles? I suppose anything is possible, but not for me. I've worked too hard to keep weight off back there. I leave the store empty-handed. The secret still escapes me.

My curiosity unslaked, I call up the Victoria's Secret number (1-800-HER-GIFT) and am referred to corporate headquarters in Columbus, Ohio. It turns out to be the headquarters of The Limited, Leslie Wexner's colossally successful empire, in which Victoria's Secret is only one of nineteen colonies—among the others are Express, Lane Bryant (large sizes), Abercrombie & Fitch, and Henri Bendel. Talking to Wexner himself is out of the question, I am told. He doesn't give interviews. But Kimber Perfect, The Limited's public-relations person, does.

"Was the name Victoria's Secret Mr. Wexner's idea?" I ask Ms. Perfect.

"No. It was a chain of three or four stores that he bought in 1982."

"Whom did he buy it from?"

"Oh, um, some man called Ray, or was it Roy? Something like that. My phone is ringing. I've got to go."

"One more quick question. Did he start it in London? I notice there's a London address on the catalog."

"No. I think the stores were in California."

Over the next two weeks, I find that The Limited is more secretive than Queen Victoria herself. When I do get through to the two women presidents, Cynthia Fedus, president of Victoria's Secret Catalogue, and Grace Nichols, president of Victoria's Secret Stores, both talk confidently about "affordable luxury," "indulgence buying," and merchandise that is "evocative but not provocative," but they don't lead me any closer to Victoria or her secret. I can't figure out the London address on the catalog, No. 10 Margaret Street. I'm told that it's an office, not a store: part of the overall image, no doubt. Although another Victoria's Secret publicist says of the founder, Roy Raymond, "I think he's dead," I do manage to track him down. He turns out to be alive and well and living in San Francisco, which is where Victoria's Secret was born.

A young hotshot with a brand-new MBA from Stanford, Raymond started Victoria's Secret in 1977 with forty thousand dollars. His mom did the bookkeeping, and his pop set up the computerized inventory system. The concept was simplicity itself. Men were embarrassed to buy lingerie for their wives or girlfriends, Raymond decided, because the only outlets for such items were "corsetiere" salons in department stores. These were forbidding places to men—lairs for women only. After studying the market for eight months, Raymond opened his first shop in a Palo Alto mall. His wife was behind the counter, and the atmosphere was friendly. "The stores were designed to make men feel comfortable, so we used dusty rose and dark wood," he tells me. "Private, fanciful, a little bit sexy." The name came from the decor, which was "Victorian sitting room, very much in the old San Francisco mode."

He also put out a catalog not unlike the current one. The main difference is that Raymond was selling high-quality, rather expensive lingerie—Lejaby, Dior, Hanro—considerably more up-market than what you find there today and decidedly more so than Frederick's of Hollywood. "We were very careful to set ourselves apart from that," Raymond says. "They were the only other lingerie catalog. It was a good three years before they decided to compete with us. They came up with Private Moments, eight stores in southern California, which was a direct run at Victoria's Secret." Subsequently, Frederick's took on a new CEO and totally changed its image. "Victoria's Secret woke us up," says Ellen Appel, that company's public-relations consultant. Frederick's still features musical underwear and backless lingerie, but it's shooting for "mainstream America" now, and instead of Vargas-inspired drawings of long-legged, big-busted bimbos, its catalog shows photographs of realistically shaped bimbos in pastel décolletage.

Victoria's Secret did well under Raymond. By 1982 he had five stores and annual sales of $6 million. "We were growing very rapidly and needed backing," he told me. It was at this point that The Limited made him an offer he couldn't refuse. Wexner wanted to take the business up to somewhere between seven hundred and a thousand stores. Raymond didn't want to be involved in that big an operation, so he sold the boutiques, the concept, and the name for a million dollars' worth of The Limited stock (plus other benefits that he's obliged to keep Raymond's Secret) and went on to other things.

The growth of Victoria's Secret under Wexner has been astonishing. In 1990 sales rocketed to $900 million. Wexner's goal is $1.5 billion for the stores by the mid-1990s. The catalog employs more than six hundred operators, who take calls twenty-four hours a day, every day, at three hundred telephone stations in Columbus, Ohio.

On Sunday I dial 1-800-HER-GIFT.

"Hello," comes the friendly and efficient-sounding voice. "I'm Jennifer, your fashion consultant for today. What would you like to start with?"

I refer her to page five in the current catalog, item C, the "whisper-light . . . sheer . . . watercolour floral print chiffon . . . baby doll with buttons in front and a flounced drop waist skirt," with matching panties, specially priced at twenty-five dollars. (Don't tell Gloria Steinem.)

"Oh, we're all out, but we expect another order in two weeks."

I order it anyway. Then I tell her I'd like to try the underpants on page fourteen, in white. They're the only ones I can see that are cut like underpants. She says they're out of white, and I can't order any because the item has been discontinued. The remaining colors are quite ghastly, but I order two in black for twenty-four dollars.

"You get two free with that," she chirps.

So I order two purple-ground floral prints. Turning to bras, I enlist Jennifer's help in finding one in my size that doesn't clasp in front or have exaggerated push-up. White, please. It won't be in for several months. Oh, dear. Why do I bother?

What I've found is that simple white cotton nightgowns are the best bets here. They're reasonably priced, well cut, and durable—"affordable luxury." I own about five or six, and I wear them all the time. The underwear is less satisfactory, but I keep ordering it anyway. So, okay, what *is* the secret? Why do I and millions of others (male and female) keep building Wexner's empire? It's partly convenience we're buying, but more than that, I think it's the concept. Underneath it all, we're hooked on romance, with a discreet yet not too discreet hint of forbidden fruits. For too many of us, the secret goal is to be sexy *and* demure, ultrafeminine and madly desirable; we're caught between Queen Victoria and Brigitte Bardot. That's my secret, anyway. A sociologist might explain all this to everybody's satisfaction and bore us to death in the process. But who cares? I can hardly wait for my whisperlight baby doll to arrive.

April 1992

manolo's mules

Last night I dreamt I went to Manolo again. Manolo Blahnik, that is, the prince of shoe designers, the man whose exquisitely shaped and opulently upholstered footwear can make any woman's legs look beautiful, feminine, and seductive. The funny thing was, I had never been to Manolo. I've spent most of my life trying to make my own legs beautiful, feminine, and seductive by other means; for the last six months, this has meant working out every day with a personal trainer and punishing my legs on a stationary bicycle. How much more pleasant it would be, I thought lazily, to achieve the same effect through Manolo's magic.

Dreams sometimes come true. Through the miracle of journalism, I am covering the Meet Manolo Blahnik event in Beverly Hills, where Manolo is introducing his new line at the recently opened Blahnik boutique in Neiman Marcus. The man turns out to be as effervescent and surprising as his shoes—an immaculately groomed, dazzlingly animated, medium-tall man in a double-breasted Savile Row suit. He tells me he has been dreading this moment. "I've been so *nervous*," he says, "but now that I see you, I feel much better." The words tumble out in quick bursts, punctuated by arpeggios of laughter; his accent is charming but indecipherable—one part Czech, one part Spanish, eight parts Manolo. We can't talk much at the moment, because Manolo is besieged by admirers. Pretty girls want him to sign their shoes—he does it with a black felt-tip pen, up under the heel, where it won't get scuffed. Los Angeles is Blahnik mad. Madonna loves him. "His shoes are wonderful," she has said, "and they last longer than sex." Cher, Julia Roberts, Geena Davis, Ellen Barkin, Whitney Houston, Sigourney Weaver, Winona Ryder, Carol Burnett, Raquel Welch, and Anjelica Huston all buy his shoes. "Miss Huston and Miss Davis are my two favorite actresses in America at the moment—and Madonna and Ellen Barkin. Those four I think are the most click click. Anjelica in *The Grifters*—God bless her with that wig and my shoes on, too."

"Annette Bening also wears your shoes," says George Malkemus, Manolo's ever-present business partner in America.

"I couldn't care less," Manolo flings back. "Anjelica's the one. *Oh-h-h-h-h*. She's the most perfect thing. She's like a piece of sculpture."

Although Manolo's conquest of America is fairly recent, he's been a hit in London since 1972, when Bianca Jagger, Loulou de La Falaise, and Marisa Berenson started wearing his outrageously original high-heeled platforms and sandals with green suede straps that climbed the leg like vines (they were festooned with red suede cherries at the top). Manolo is a long way from platforms today. The shoes he does now are lighter than air. He has pioneered the no-shoe shoe. His brocades and silk velvets and bejeweled fantasies manage to be flamboyant and delicate in the same breath. Bill Blass, Geoffrey Beene, Carolina Herrera, and Isaac Mizrahi demand Manolo's shoes for their shows. He has brought the mule out of the bedroom and into the great world.

"I've got twenty-four pairs of your mules, and it's not enough," an ardent customer rushes up to tell Manolo. His Pilgrim-buckle suede mule is a must for L.A. women. There is a round table at Neiman Marcus entirely filled with them; their opulent linings and rainbow colors would make any Pilgrim run for cover—no new austerity for Manolo Blahnik. His shoes cost plenty (from $385 for a suede penny loafer to $1,200 for a jewel-encrusted bootee or a thigh-high doeskin boot), but that doesn't stop his fans. Sales in this country now approach $7 million a year. "It's the most phenomenal thing in shoes, ever," a Neiman Marcus shoe buyer tells me. "They sell as if they're being given away. They're recession-proof."

A Neiman Marcus salesperson comes up to Manolo and says, "You're one of the ABCs."

"ABCs?" Manolo asks.

"What sells in L.A.—Armani, Blahnik, and Chanel."

After five hours of Meet Manolo Blahnik, he breaks loose and we head back to the Beverly Wilshire, four blocks away. He walks with a curious gliding motion, his head well forward, his blue-green eyes taking in everything. On Wilshire Boulevard we pass a young blonde in beige shorts and beige suede mules. "Look. My shoes," cries Manolo. "She's *gre-a-t*. Wonderfully clean. Groomed to death. Shorts with a mule—I love that. Why not? Mules is forever. Are forever. I think Dawdie should need a mule, George. But a high mule, with buckle. So get one before I forget. If I was a woman, I'd be all the time in mules."

The beige girl turns around, smiles, and waves to us. "I *lo-o-ve* that beige girl," Manolo says. "I don't know her, George. Do you think she knows me?"

Manolo was born forty-nine years ago in the Canary Islands. His father was Czech; his mother's family owned the banana plantation on which he grew up. He and his younger sister, Evangeline, who now runs the Manolo Blahnik shop in London, were tutored at home until the age of fourteen, when they were packed off to Swiss boarding schools. He learned a lot of languages, read a lot of books, saw tons of movies, attended the University of Geneva, spent a formative year in Paris, and landed in London in 1969, where his real life began. "I was possessed by London. It was post-Beatles and all that nonsense, and to me the city seemed very exotic." He tells me this at Le Dôme restaurant on Sunset Boulevard, where the three of us (George included) are having lunch. Manolo, who is allergic to wine but very partial to sweets, orders a second vanilla ice cream with hot fudge sauce, over George's protest. "Why not, George? I indulge myself in a few wonderful things."

In addition to sweets, Manolo's indulgences include living quarters, dogs, and underwear.

He has a chic flat in Kensington, a noble nineteenth-century house in Bath, and two houses in the Canaries—one in the old town of Santa Cruz de la Palma and another up in the mountains (it came with its own mule). Seven dogs call him master; one of them, a Scottie called Tulo, who is named after the Roman poet Catullus, walks him to the office every day in London. His bed linens come from Ghidoli in Milan, which also supplies the Vatican. "The most extraordinary feeling, the well-being feeling for me, is being absolutely, all-the-time groomed. My constant worry is to have fabulous underwear. You never know if you're going to be run over by a car. Sex isn't important. Beautiful underwear is." His underwear comes from Biraghi in Milan, Charvet in Paris, and Bowring Arundel in London, but "nothing beats Brooks Brothers in New York," he adds.

Manolo detests running shoes, and he's not too fond of blue jeans. This may have something to do with his having started out as a jeans buyer for Feathers, a trendy London boutique of the early 1970s. At that time he thought he might become a set designer—he has always been mad for movies and theater. But when he showed his portfolio to Diana Vreeland on a trip to New York in 1971, her eye lighted on the shoes that people were wearing in his set designs. Both Vreeland and China Machado told him he should be designing shoes. He already had designed some men's shoes for Zapata, a tiny shop in London's Chelsea district started by some friends. Back in London, he designed a line of shoes for Ossie Clark's new spring collection—Ossie Clark was one of the most popular London designers of the moment—and suddenly he was off and running. Zapata, which he bought from the previous owner, became the Manolo Blahnik boutique, and Manolo Blahnik became a name to reckon with.

There were some problems with those early shoes. "They were shoes with high heels and crepe soles. The heels were rubber. Of course, they had metal spines [he pronounces it "speens"], but they weren't what I call very safe. They wobbled a bit. Those girls at Ossie Clark's show were teetering in those high rubber shoes and falling off, and it was hys-*ter*-ia. I always jump into things without knowing. It's like everything in my life. I didn't know anything about shoes, but I know there is some element there that I like. It was like a choice, but it wasn't a choice. I jump."

A slim blond girl with a truly exceptional bosom struts by our table. Manolo breaks off, riveted. "Is it real, George? Unbelievable. I'm not shockable, but this is kind of shocking."

For quite a few years, Manolo's shoes looked great but were notoriously uncomfortable. In time, though, he worked out the comfort equation. "My philosophy is three things: comfort, quality, and design. No compromise for quality. Design can be good or not good, but it's got to be *fantastic*. But comfort is the most important. It took me ten years, and even now I'm still learning. You never achieve perfection, but you get near it. A marriage of many things—balance, grace, lightness. I'm happy sometimes what I do, but I have things to master still."

In George's room at the Beverly Wilshire, I get him to look at my "feets," as he calls them—my ridiculously small, size four or four and a half feet(s) that are impossible to find shoes for. He prescribes mules. "Oh, a mule would be heaven. Oh-oh-oh-oh." He sketches several different mules for me on the hotel stationery. "It's fine for a small foot, and you walk differently with a mule. Immediately. [He demonstrates, flouncing across the carpet.] You'll see. Your husband will faint. [Avalanche of stage giggles.] I think that's what people tend to call sexy. I don't understand the word *sexy* very much, but I suppose it's the way you walk. You know something? I've been doing mules for donkey years now, and suddenly, three years ago, people started to want more mules, more mules, and more mules. This year, we're selling mules in velvet, in silver, in silk, in chiffon, in flannel.

"I don't like to use animal stuff," he says. "Leather is animal. I really love beautiful, opulent fabrics. I really love paisley—quilted paisley outside, waterproof, of course, and inside the most exquisite Russian sable. But very pale, almost pinky sable. How divine that would be." Sable is an animal, of course, but consistency is for nerds. Manolo himself is wearing crocodile driving shoes of his own design. "Crocodiles should be killed, because they are the only animal that is very, very cruel.

"If you're a good girl, in Milan you'll get some mules."

Manolo has invited me to come to Milan, where his shoes are made. We are bosom buddies now.

"Ambrogio. Am-*bro*-gio!"

We enter the factory in Parabiago, north of

Milan, where Manolo's haute couture shoes are made. Sounds of sewing and stitching machinery. About thirty employees, most of them doing handwork. Ambrogio, a sixtyish master craftsman in a beige brown smock, comes out and gives me a warm handshake. This operation is like a family business. The factory turns out about five finished pairs of shoes a day.

"This is how I work," Manolo tells me. "First, I sketch. It comes to me like a puff. I materialize it with pencil or brush, and then the next thing is I have to sculpt it out of wood." To my amazement, it appears that Manolo Blahnik does most of the manual work on the original models for all of his designs. He takes a square block of wood, outlines the shape of a heel in pencil, sculpts it on a machine, smooths it with sandpaper and a file. "Manufacturing shoes is not like dresses. It takes a long time. The first sample is all by hand. Everything has got to be mathematically perfect, and of course the technicians do the final grading." The result is a closely guarded secret. (At lunch today at Savini, his favorite restaurant in Milan, Manolo surreptitiously slid the model for next winter's heel out of his coat pocket to show me; he carries it with him at all times, he said, because fashion spies are everywhere. "This season's heel has already been ripped off. Espionage. Es-pi-o-nage!")

The rest of the process is even more time-consuming. He often spends three days on a single shoe, cutting, drawing, gluing, smoothing, recutting, reworking, perfecting. "Exact, exact, exact," he says, "or else it's a failure." He shows me a sketch for a cream-colored sandal for next spring, satin covered and beaded, called Udaipur. "The beading is done in India. Do you realize what that costs? Ladies take whole mornings to do this, and people complain it's expensive. It's not expensive at all. *Come o-o-on*. Udaipur, what a stupid name. I love stupid names."

Manolo gets the names for his shoes from the places he's been, movies he's seen, or books he's read. He's a tremendous reader. One recent model, the Sedara, is a Sicilian name that he took from Lampedusa's classic Italian novel, *The Leopard*. "Each shoe has some reference. Everything is pregnant with meanings."

His designs often come to him while he is in the Uffizi, the Prado, and the Metropolitan Museum of Art. "You go to a museum with him and what he always notices is the feet," says George. "Those *huge* canvases by David at the Louvre," says Manolo. "Always the thing that gets into my mind is those feets. And all those beautiful shoes in the Prado. We've been going downhill since the eighteenth century."

Manolo takes out his ancient Hermès diary and shows me a picture of a Greek soldier he cut from an airline magazine. (There is also a photo of Diana Vreeland.) "Look at those shoes," he says, pointing to the upturned toes of the evzone. "Aren't they ravishing? We are so poor now, we haven't got imagination. *We are dressed in uniforms of grayness and sadness*. Why shouldn't every woman wear jewels in the middle of the day? After all, this is a time of horror, so you should dare to wear anything. Be yourself and bead yourself."

He suddenly sits down at a big worktable, pops a piece of anise candy into his mouth, and dashes off a large red-ink drawing of a mule with his signature rakishly curved heel and red-suede-covered cork balls sprouting up on wires. "This is for you, Dawdie." Then he tells me to take off my shoes. He has me stand on a piece of drawing paper so that he can trace the outlines of both my feet(s). My mules will be ready in two weeks, he says. He also tells me the secret of how to keep my feet happy: pumice stone. "Every bath hour. Just plain water, pumice stone, and talcum powder. And a little clear varnish on the nails, or else red red."

We walk between the worktables where elderly ladies are handstitching pleated silk crepe for mules. "Ah, Signora," Manolo says, taking the needle and thread from one woman's hands to demonstrate the extra-tiny stitching he wants. At another table he shows how the glacé kid lining is applied to a shoe. "If the skin is too thin, too breakable, we have to line it with material and then squeeze it, press it, and iron it. It's prettier inside than outside. It breaks my heart when people say these shoes are expensive. I try to convey a feeling of opulence, of abundance. You know, ribbons, wonderful silk satin, crushed velvet, pleating, embroidery, jewels. You have to have everything with generosity."

Limousining through Milan en route to another factory, he takes umbrage at the overpermed long hair of the Milanese girls. "Milan has been totally polluted by women's hair," he complains. "I'm talking about sheepskin hair, *mouton* hair. Oh God, I hate that hair. I really like clean hair. Look at those two children—she's fifteen, she's twelve, and they've got the victim hair already.

Milanese victim hair. I wouldn't mind taking a match and just—or a pair of pinking shears. Doing a favor to the nation."

We pass the Grand Hotel, where he always stays when he's in Milan. This time, it's closed for repairs. He is staying at the Principe di Savoia, quite unhappily. The elevator doesn't work well, and he has changed rooms three times in eight days.

An attractive girl in a small sports car pulls up next to us at a light. "She reminds me of Nastassia Kinski, that girl. Hi-i-i," he calls over. No response. "She's not very friendly. Come on, you should smile. You don't know, maybe I'm a movie director."

Today's factory, in the small town of Vigevano, is where Manolo's shoes *du jour* get made. Sandals, street shoes, boots. Although two factories might sound like big business, Manolo's operation has remained small and exclusive. "I never was and never will be interested in mass," he says. "Never like Charles Jourdan." He's thinking of opening one more boutique, on the Continent (probably Paris), which with his stores in London, New York, and Hong Kong will be quite enough, thank you.

Inside the factory they're working feverishly on Annie Oakley—a boot that Manolo is doing for Isaac Mizrahi's upcoming show, only ten days off. "George came from New York and said Isaac wants a little Victorian boot—western Victorian. In a second I got it. I thought of Sophia Loren in George Cukor's film *Heller in Pink Tights*, where in one scene Sophia is a chanteuse in a saloon. It's an exquisite little boot. If Isaac doesn't like it, I kill him." He picks up one of the cotton laces for the boot, smells it, bites it, tastes it. "I want it long, l-o-o-o-o-ng," he croons. "I want it to wrap around the leg like a monkey."

Manolo is a sensory virtuoso. He savors each passing moment and often comments on its look, feel, or smell. His personal scent is Knize Ten, a citron-smelling Austrian cologne that his father and grandfather used. "You know something?" he confides. "I don't buy magazines that give you whiffs of some nasty perfume they're advertising. Ooopla. I can't bear it. You know which one I'm talking about. My lips are sealed."

Manolo shows me summer sandals—a whole galaxy of colors and fabrics, most named after Italian movie stars. "This is what the girls want. So comfortable and so sexy. It's a gold mule called Vitti, like Monica Vitti." There is also a Loren and a Magnani. Another, called Muna, has a tiny ball to go between the first and the second toes and a discreet plastic strap across the top of the foot. "This is the first time I used plastic," Manolo says. "I don't like plastic shoes, because you can see all the toes squashed, and everything is so unattractive. Perspiration. But in this one, it looks like you have nothing but a little ball.

"The last ten years has been heavy, heavy work. More and more and more. But I've become aware of what shoes are now in this kind of modern society."

"What are they?" I ask.

"Entertainment. Total entertainment. A sort of link between my personality and many, many other people. Quality is always going to be paramount. But on top of that, the shoe has got to be an escape. You put a shoe on, and it's like *Cinderella*. You look down and say, How lovely, how dainty, how pointy, what fabulous color, what beautiful embroidery, what wonderful stitches. My shoes are fleeting moments. My biggest kick in life, if I only achieve one thing, is to entertain people."

We drive from the factory to the old square in the middle of Vigevano, something he's been wanting to show me. It is late afternoon, and the church bell is ringing. "This is Italy at its best," he says. "This emptiness, these wonderful sounds, this architecture. *What else do you wa-a-a-ant?* To me, it's one of the most perfect squares in Italy. It's only a village, and it's so grand and so fabulous and so elegant. I'm in heaven here."

Back in New York, I'm pumicing my feet when I should be riding the stationary bike. My Manolo mules have just arrived. How pointy! How dainty! How beautiful, feminine, and seductive. And how *com*fortable. I'm learning to walk with a new, muley strut. My husband is sure to faint.

March 1992

pearls

She sits at her writing desk in profile, one hand to her cheek as she turns to receive the letter her maid is bringing her—a beautiful young woman in a yellow fur-trimmed jacket, with some of the loveliest pearls in Western art. The mistress of Vermeer's *Mistress and Maid*, in the Frick Museum, wears a pearl necklace, a rope of pearls wound around and through her blond chignon, and a huge, voluptuous teardrop pearl earring. Every time I see her, I wish I could look like that. Is it the way the pearls seem to gather light and play it back so lustrously over her smooth cheek? Is there any other jewel that can convey both purity and sensuality in the same breath? Vermeer, who painted pearls so miraculously, must have felt the same way about them that I do.

I've learned a thing or two about pearls during the last few weeks. They have come back into favor, rebounding from a major slump that cut sales from nearly one billion a year in the late 1980s to something like $700 million last year.

The pearl's age-old appeal is reasserting itself in all sorts of jazzy new designs, where the emphasis is on informality, ingenuity, and irreverence. Pearl showers raining from platinum wires; huge, misshapen ("baroque") pearls used as rings; shoes and boots festooned with rattling clumps of pink freshwater "stick" and "rondelle" pearls; black pearls intertwined with white pearls—the variations seem endless. The classic one, two, or three-strand pearl necklace will never go out of style, of course, but at the top end of the market, megapearl necklaces made out of giant South Sea pearls the size of Ping-Pong balls are all the rage, while at the low end unsuspecting neophytes buy $99 pearl necklaces—with genuine cultured pearls, not fakes—from Kmart and QVC.

For years, I thought that cultured pearls were not really real. Ever since Kokichi Mikimoto's patented process captured the market in the 1920s, though, natural pearls have become rarer and rarer—they now account for less than 0.1% of sales worldwide. Moreover, it's virtually impossible to tell the difference between them and the cultured variety. A natural pearl occurs when an irritant of some sort—a parasite, a tiny fish, or a crab—lodges in the soft body of the oyster, and the oyster protects itself by wrapping that irritant in layer after layer of nacre, the iridescent substance with which it also coats the interior of its shell. In a cultured pearl, the irritant is man-made, but the rest of the process is exactly the same. Pearl snobs call this artificial insemination, but a test-tube baby is still a baby, and a cultured pearl is still a pearl. "I defy someone who is not a top-notch pearl expert to tell the difference between a cultured pearl and a natural one," says John Loring, the design director of Tiffany's. "And I have a suspicion that without modern technology, even the expert can't be sure."

There's a wide range of quality in cultured pearls, of course, and the ones you buy at Kmart are not going to last long. Their nacre may be only .05 millimeters thick, because they have been in the oyster for four months or less, and it cracks or wears off in no time. If you want to be safe, go to Tiffany or Cartier or Mikimoto, and you'll be sure of getting pearls that have luxuriated in the oyster for at least two or three years, acquiring a thousand or more layers of nacre; their luster will hold up, with proper use and care, for several generations. (Unlike diamonds, pearls are not forever; no pearl holds its luster for more than five hundred years, although if the pearl is large enough and good enough, an expert technician can peel off the chalky-looking outer skin to reveal a newly gleaming underlayer.) Even at Tiffany, though, the pearl fancier is no longer limited to polite and ever so dignified pearl strands and stud earrings. Elsa Perretti, who gave us diamonds by the yard, has now come out with pearls by the yard, and she's also doing rings with the irregular-shaped pearls that are referred to in the trade as baroque. Tiffany offers the large South Sea pearls as well as the smaller Japanese variety—you can pick up one triple strand of whoppers for $1.85 million—but at Tiffany, as at Mikimoto, the main emphasis is still on classic necklaces made of perfectly round, pea-sized pearls in the virginal white or slightly pinkish hue. For the wilder innovations in pearl jewelry, you have to go elsewhere.

"A single strand or a double strand of pearls

is not really where it's at," says Janis Savitt, "even though everyone should have one." Savitt has done a pearl choker with a diamond lightning bolt in the front. She hangs different-size pearls on an invisible threadlike chain so they look like they're floating, and impales them on platinum neck bands, with other pearls dropping down at odd intervals. She is doing a "whip" necklace with no clasp, a long string of pearls, graduated from very small to very large, that you just wind around your neck, wrist, or waist, or anywhere you want, and loop it through. Savitt has also done a pearl necklace that's like a rope, thousands of tiny seed pearls woven by hand. "It's the modern alternative to a regular strand of pearls," she says.

The irrepressible Manolo Blahnik, who has often used fake pearls on his famous shoes, is now smothering them in the real thing. "There is an *enormous* desire for pearls at the moment," he says. "Because, you see, there's been too much fake stuff, fake diamonds, fake everything. In the age of faxes, people do not want facsimiles anymore. They want the real thing. Besides, we have the end of the millennium, so why not bring back the opulence that we need?" Manolo's new evening slippers will have scads of magenta-colored, sticklike freshwater pearls (interspersed with flattish rondelles) climbing up the instep, where they will make quite a clatter. One of the boots in his next collection will have baroque pearls hanging like Christmas baubles. "Pearls give a gloss, a certain refinement, even if you're just a trashy girl," says Manolo. "I'm not interested in matron. No, no, no. I'm talking about young kiddies with pearls. Jeans with pearls. Trash with pearls. Any kind of woman can wear pearls. A dwarf, a native from Tierra del Fuego, anybody. It doesn't matter if you have a problem with your body, if you're ugly or pretty. Of course, on a dwarf, the larger the pearl the better. A dwarf must wear a huge, black South Sea pearl. If you're older, you need even more pearls. Pearls make you feel alive."

At Verdura, the perennial fount of modern jewelry design, I saw a $65,000 three-strand black-and-white pearl necklace that ties like a scarf, with three delicious tassels. To my amazement, I learned that it was designed by the late Duke of Verdura thirty-five years ago—*plus ça change*. . . . Verdura president Ward Landrigan let me try on Marie Antoinette's luscious fifty-three-pearl necklace, the one Barbara Hutton used to own; it's back on the market for more than $2 million, and wearing it made me feel a little weird. The natural pearls haven't lost any of their luster after two hundred years, but I don't want to lose my head the way Marie Antoinette did. Verdura has influenced everyone, including Chanel, who hired him to design her jewelry in 1926. Chanel has recently gone into real jewelry on its own, and about a third of the collection features pearls. Coco Chanel did more than anyone else to popularize fake pearls in the twenties, before Mikimoto's cultured pearl revolution. She mixed them with real pearls in an irreverent, breezy way that anticipated what's going on right now. Ever since, Chanel's line of costume jewelry has leaned heavily on the faux variety—glass beads coated on the inside with fish oil paint, and filled with paste—but make no mistake, Chanel loved the real thing and had plenty of it, and the company is sure she would have approved of this new venture. I certainly approve of it when I see some examples at their corporate office. There are "quilted" necklaces, bracelets, earrings, and rings, in which fabulous pearls are interlaced with gold (and diamonds, if you like)—they have the intricate, beautifully worked rightness of a Chanel suit. The quilted necklace has 193 perfectly matched pearls and costs $215,000; the ring, without diamonds, is $3,400, and feels as though it belongs on my hand (someday, maybe). I also love the Chanel "pompom" earrings, with a dozen or so pearl-bearing tassels that jangle alluringly. "We play to win in this company," Chanel's chief executive officer, Ari Koppelman, confides to me. "This business about the nineties no longer wanting luxury goods is nonsense. The first half of the nineties is over, and it's clear that the gears have been shifted again."

Elizabeth Gage, the English jeweler, takes a suite at the Carlyle for a couple of days once a year, and the ladies come and shop. She uses a lot of pearls in heavy, medieval-looking rings, brooches, earrings, and so forth—jewelry with impact. She's done a spectacular lion's head pin carved out of bicolored tourmaline, with a ruby and diamond collar; a huge baroque South Sea pearl dangles from the bottom. It's one of a kind, and it's $20,000. "I've always loved big baroque pearls," she tells me. "I don't like them, I love them. No two are alike. It doesn't have any pretense to roundness, but it has a wonderful shape. In the Renaissance, they used baroque pearls for the tummies of mermaids or men." Angela Pintaldi also goes in for big baroques. She's a young Milanese designer who sells through Diego Della Valle on 57th Street.

What's unique about her work is that she uses only natural pearls, humongous ones from the waters off Australia, the baroquer the better. When she makes a choker, it takes her up to seven or eight years to collect the pearls. She sells to Mercedes Bass, Jane Wrightsman, Marie-Hélène Rothschild, and other ladies who really know their nacre, the kind of customers whom Verdura depends on. Although Pintaldi rarely uses gold anymore, she makes a fantastic ring with a pearl the size of a walnut, held in place by tiny sculptured men, women, and children. "The pearl represents the world," she says, "and they're trying to save it from pollution."

Not all the young designers are going in for baroque shapes and new concepts. Mark Jacobs, who started designing jewelry a year ago, likes his pearls round, uniform, and perfectly matched. "I'm not going to reinvent the pearl necklace," he says. "The material itself is classic, so it defies being trendy. It doesn't really matter what you do with a pearl. It's like a cashmere sweater. To me, a diamond is not last season and a pearl this season. That's old-fashioned magazine mentality." He has a point, I'd say. After five thousand years of glorious desirability, does the pearl really need reinventing?

The pearl, alone among fine gems, comes to us complete and perfect. It requires no cutting or faceting or polishing, and its famous luster, which is simply light refracted through transparent layers of nacre, is the oyster's unwitting gift. There is a simple test for luster: If you can see a clear image of your face in the pearl, it's top quality. No wonder we love them. The Queen of Sheba basked in them. Cleopatra bet Mark Antony that she could spend more than 10 million sesterces for a single meal, and won the bet by dissolving a single pearl earring in her glass of wine and then drinking it. (Since wine doesn't dissolve pearls, she probably had a slave grind it up first.) Queen Elizabeth I of England, the Virgin Queen, was so avid for pearls that she covered every dress, crown, and wig she owned with them: on public occasions she wore seven or more ropes of nutmeg-size pearls at a time, the longest of which extended to her knees. Maysie Plant, the wife of New York banker Morton F. Plant, traded her Renaissance palace on Fifth Avenue to Pierre Cartier in 1917 for a two-strand pearl necklace—valued at a million dollars—that had taken him several years to assemble. The house has been Cartier's New York headquarters ever since; the necklace, sold at Sotheby's in 1957, brought $151,000. All right, so pearls are not such a great investment, but does that make us love them less? Not at all. In fact, because natural pearls today are worth only about a tenth of what they were before 1929, and because thieves have a hard time distinguishing between real ones and fakes, they are probably the safest jewel to wear and to own. In the $1.9 million jewelry heist at Tiffany's in September 1994, not a single piece of pearl jewelry was taken.

This is not to say that pearls don't bring high prices. In the past few years, according to Sotheby's jewelry expert John Block, "pearls have been among the most expensive things at auction. We've sold two cultured pearl necklaces for more than $2 million each—world-record prices for any pearl necklace, natural or cultured." Block assigns a lot of the credit for this to Salvador Assael, a pearl in the rough if ever there was one. Assael literally made the current market for the outsize South Sea pearls, including the increasingly popular black pearl, whose cultivation, processing, and marketing he largely controls. "We invented the eighteen-fifteen necklace," Assael says, "the million-dollar pearl necklace. It didn't exist before me." He's talking about a choker of pearls whose size runs from fifteen millimeters in back to eighteen in front. "Larger than that, it's two million," he says. (A twenty-sixteen version sold at Sotheby's in October 1992 for $2,310,000.) Some people feel that pearls this big are just a touch, well, vulgar. "It's like hanging money around your neck," says one respected jewelry expert. "It's not about jewelry anymore, it's about power." Barry Kieselstein-Cord, one of the top jewelry designers, disagrees with this. "You can look vulgar with diamonds," he says, "but you can never look vulgar with pearls." A number of prominent New York women have bought Assael's power chokers, but I'm not supposed to give their names—according to gossip columnist Suzy, who sometimes wears a sub-million-dollar Assael job herself, it's not polite to identify the owner of a super gem. I can only say that one of them is the queen of New York residential real estate, and another's name is a combination of an expensive car and a fish.

What else did I find out about pearls? Each year's crop is different, and as with wine, some years are better than others. Salvador Assael is jubilant about his 1994 black pearl crop, which produced the largest specimen ever found—nineteen millimeters. The Sultan of Brunei is reportedly negotiating with Assael for a $12 million pearl necklace, which would make it the most expensive ever. (I don't mind mentioning the Sultan of Brunei, who recently paid more than a million dollars for a one-carat red diamond.) Americans like their pearls pinkish white, Japanese prefer the silver-green kind, South Americans favor creme or gold. A great many pink pearls have appeared in the American market in recent years, and it's pretty clear that chemical dyes have been used to give some of them a better blush. Pearl processing is a highly secretive operation, and a risky one. Typhoons, red tides, and other natural calamities can wipe out entire crops. Mikimoto, which claims that only the top 3 percent of its cultured pearls reach the stores, has its own grading system, from A to AAA, but plenty of mediocre pearls get marketed from places like China, which exerts no quality controls at all. In Japan, poor quality pearls often get ground up and sold as medicine (aphrodisiacs, mostly), face powder, and miracle anti-wrinkle face cream. Pearl nacre is 90 percent calcium carbonate—the main ingredient in Tums and Rolaids. Kokichi Mikimoto is said to have eaten a pearl a day, and he lived to be ninety-five.

Pearls should be worn, not kept in a vault (or eaten). They love to be next to skin, but they react badly to heat, perfume, hair spray, and perspiration. So you should wash them in soap and water, and dry them without rubbing. Angela Pintaldi's grandmother taught her to keep her pearls in a covered box of white rice, after wearing them, to draw out the impurities and bad vibrations. A pearl necklace should be restrung at least once a year, because the silk thread gets dirty and disturbs the pearl's delicate equilibrium. It almost sounds as though a pearl is a living thing, which is certainly the way it looks in Vermeer's painting.

Oh, and pearls are the birthstone of people born in June, like me. Someday, maybe.

the winter coat

It's the middle of summer and it's scorching hot. To make things worse, one minute I'm being buttoned into fake tiger fur, and five minutes later I'm wrapped up like a mummy in heavy gray mohair. This is not a bad dream. I'm in New York City, trying to buy my first winter coat. Believe it or not, I have never bought one before. I've escaped it because my mother has always given me her castoffs. But I simply can't wear one of my mother's hand-me-down furs anymore, especially since my recently acquired eight-year-old stepdaughter is an animal-rights activist.

Actually, I tried to buy a coat last winter, when I was cold, but the only coats in the stores in January and February are beach robes. I was told to come back in July—when all the designer coats start coming in. So here I am. But the trouble is, there are so many different kinds of coats to choose from that I am totally confused. I hate shopping. Help! At this point, right on cue, I remember all those department store advertisements for "personal shoppers," who supposedly serve your every need. Why not give them a try?

I call six department stores—Bergdorf's, Bloomingdale's, Barney's, Bendel's, Saks, and Macy's—and ask for the personal-shopping department in each one. They all have personal shoppers in one form or another, and each asks me some obvious questions—my dress size, my hair color, my height, and so forth. The only instruction I give is no real fur, please—but fake is okay.

At Saks, when I ask for a personal shopper, the operator connects me with the Fifth Avenue Club. "Do you want to join the Fifth Avenue Club?" the clipped female voice asks.

"No. I mean, I don't think so. I want to speak to a personal shopper who can help me buy a winter coat."

"I'm going to transfer you to the One on One Service."

"What's the One on One Service?"

"For one-item shoppers like you."

Before I can find out what the Fifth Avenue Club can do for me, she's gone, and a new voice says, "One on One." After a few minutes' conversation, Gertruda Cheng, my very own personal shopper, says, "You probably want petite."

"I hate the word *petite*," I reply. It makes me feel smaller than my five feet two and a quarter inches. She says she'll get together some possibilities, and we set a date. (I never really did find out about the Fifth Avenue Club, except that it seems to be for big spenders, Trumps and other red-carpet types.)

I make all my appointments for next Monday and Tuesday. My first is at Bergdorf Goodman.

I walk in with great confidence, because for the first time in my life I know exactly where I'm going in a department store. Straight to my personal shopper on the sixth floor. "Would you like to go for a walk on the floor?" she asks me right off. She is Judith Peterson, a neatly dressed young woman with neatly cropped hair who started as a wig-and-makeup artist in the theater and who is one of five shoppers at Bergdorf's. I am a little surprised that she doesn't have some coats waiting for me in a special dressing room. She explains that it was important for her to see me and get to know me first. "Once I've worked with you, you don't even have to come in." When we get to the designer coat floor, she takes me to the fake furs. "Do you like this?" she asks, pulling out one arm of a fake tiger Italian swing coat. In order for me to try it on, she has to unleash it from a big padlock. I want to like it, but isn't it too much coat for me? "This is not right on you," she says very directly. "It's too camp, and you're not camp." I spy another fake fur that I like by the same Italian designer and want to try it on, but she is steering me in another direction. She knows I like Saint Laurent, so she shows me Saint Laurent's new leather coats. "Leather is not for me," I say. No argument. She takes me to a black cloth coat made especially for Bergdorf's that has fake lamb trim and big frog closings. This one is padlocked, too. (As a matter of fact, every coat I try on is securely locked, a dismal sign of the times.) She likes it on me, but we both agree that it is more of a second coat, not my main winter coat. I don't want a second coat before I get my first coat, I explain to her. She understands perfectly, and we go back to that other fake fur I wanted to try on. Like the tiger, it's a swing coat and a one-size-fits-all; but what kind of animal is it?

"Spotted cat." It has a label in it, but I can't read it. My personal shopper can't either. She asks the saleswoman in the department.

"It's Milano," the saleswoman says. But who in Milan?

"Milano," she repeats firmly, and then adds, "it's very well made."

I put it on. "That looks great on you," Judith says. And that's all she says, no hard sell. I'm late for my next personal shopper at Bloomingdale's, and I tell Judith I have to go. It's the only coat like it, and she says she'll hold it for me.

In the jungle of Bloomingdale's, all my reasons for hating to shop rain down on me. It's huge, impersonal, threatening, and even dangerous. As I reach the top of the escalator to the second floor, I'm enveloped by a double-barreled squirt of scent. "Ladies, experience Safari today by Ralph Lauren," two Waspish-looking young women in white Ralph Lauren riding pants say in unison. My allergies can't take perfume. Coughing and reeking of Safari, I stagger up to the fourth floor, behind the shoe department, where my personal shopper lives.

It looks like a cozy boutique, with dresses and suits and accessories hanging haphazardly. It's even got a boutiquey-sounding name, Hope's Corner. A relaxed and friendly looking woman of about fifty-five asks, "Can I help you?"

"I'm looking for Fran."

"Fran's with another customer right now, but I can help you. I'm Hope." When I tell her that Fran was going to help me find a coat, she says,

"Oh, so you're the one who's never bought a coat before. Come with me." Hope Golden started Hope's Corner eleven years ago; before that, she was a personal shopper at Bonwit's for twenty-five years. Hope is a pioneer. Personal shoppers (or advisers or coordinators, as some stores call them) didn't become mainstream at the department stores until recently. They've all increased their personal-shopper staffs—Saks is moving its nineteen-coordinator One on One Service to its capacious bridal suite this fall. Bergdorf's pampers its personal shoppees by serving them catered lunches as they wiggle in and out of the clothes.

Hope takes me directly to Christian Lacroix and shows me two swing coats made of mohair, one turf green with a collar and the other hot pink without a collar. "Since you don't wear makeup, the hot pink gives you a lift," she says. "And it's not overpowering." I agree. Then she takes me and the coat down one floor to nondesigner coats and fake furs, just so I can see the range of what's available. I try on a fake leopard swing by Searle, but it's not as good as my spotted cat at Bergdorf's. We go back up to the fourth floor and walk through Armani. "These muted browns, tans, and grays aren't for you," she advises. Bloomingdale's isn't so bad after all, when I'm shopping with Hope. She knows where everything is. "I start walking around the floors before nine every morning, and I keep walking until I know what's in the store." When we get back to Hope's Corner for me to try on the pink Lacroix again, there is a gaggle of women waiting for Hope's expertise. She's as calm as ever. She offers to hold the pink Lacroix for me—again, no pressure—and I'm off for my next appointment.

In the unair-conditioned taxi on the way downtown to Barney's, I think about the hot pink coat and the spotted cat. Do I want a cloth coat or an appropriation of a fur coat? Buying a coat is a big decision. More so than a dress or a suit or a skirt. It's the way you present yourself to the world every time you go outside. And it's expensive. (Every one I've tried on so far costs about seventeen hundred dollars.) How can I ever decide?

My personal shopper at Barney's is Angela Naddeo, who is cute and young and smaller than I am. She has a whole rack of coats waiting in her office for me to try on. They're all more sporty than what I had in mind—a camel hair by Calvin Klein, a peach-colored Isaac Mizrahi peacoat, and any number of other coats that look more like jackets—except for the last one: a black cloth coat by Karl Lagerfeld with velvet-trimmed pockets and collar. I like it, but it's about four sizes too big for me. Angela is sympathetic. She takes me for a walk through the other coats in the store. I see the same leopard coat by Searle that was at Bloomie's. I try on a gray cashmere bathrobe-style Zoran. Too big. On to Bendel's.

Cynthia Campbell, attractive, wearing a long French braid and a leopard chiffon blouse, is in her thirties and very personable. We meet in the middle of better dresses on the second floor, and she takes me straight to Karl Lagerfeld's niche. She pulls out a beautifully cut peach wool coat and the same black coat I just saw at Barneys—only this time it's my size. We go into a cool dressing room. We agree that the peach coat is more coat than I can handle. As I'm trying on the black coat, she leaves and comes back an instant later with a purple Lagerfeld suit jacket. "I just want you to see how well this jacket fits." Then a black Lagerfeld dress arrives. Then another Lagerfeld dress—a too-low-cut black-and-white-check job. Finally, a black Lagerfeld suit appears.

"But I want a coat."

It's six o'clock. Cynthia holds everything except the black-and-white dress until tomorrow. For some reason, the feeling is not hard sell. She's letting me know that there are more than coats in this jungle. "I tell people, 'Say you hate it or you like it when I hold something up, and then we don't waste time.'" One of her clients is Barbra Streisand; Cynthia makes house calls for her and will do the same for you.

If you're going to use a personal shopper, you have to know when to say no, and mean it. And most of them make it easy for you to do so. It's a completely free service that the stores offer because they know it pays off—in customer satisfaction. Personal shoppers will take care of your every need, from sending panty hose by messenger to your office to doing your Christmas shopping and offering advice on your love life. None of the personal shoppers I saw work on commission, so there is no need for them to push you into buying something you're not going to like. What they primarily want is for you to be a satisfied customer so you will come back. A lot of people are reluctant to try this service because they feel it's only for the ultrarich and celebrities. Not so. "I don't have too many customers who will buy the three-thousand-dollar dress," Hope Golden at Bloomingdale's told me. "If it's a two-hundred-dollar dress that somebody is looking for, I won't do it. But I will go out and shop for a forty-dollar shirt if it's for a regular customer."

That night I go home and turn the air-conditioning up to extra cool and think about the fake spotted cat and the hot pink Lacroix.

The next morning I'm at Saks when the doors open. With some difficulty, I find Gertruda Cheng in a cramped office with other One on One coordinators. We walk through the nondesigner coat section, and I spot a classic-cut camel-colored cashmere with Saks's own label. It's nice, but it's not *the* coat I've been waiting for all these years. Then on to Valentino. "Would you like to try this?" she asks me, pulling out a matte red wool coat, short but not a swinger.

The lapels are too big. "Wait here," she says, and she returns with her arms full of more coats. The Valentino floor turns into my public dressing room. First I try on the same Lacroix coat that Hope is holding for me at Bloomingdale's, only this one is tangerine. I don't like it as much as the hot pink.

"Does it come in any other color?" I ask. She says no. The downside of using a particular store's personal shopper is that you are limited to what's available in that store. I try on a deep purple Saint Laurent with big lapels and slits on both sides. After that a gray wool tuxedo-cut Ferré. Then the fake leopard I've seen at two stores already. "I'm expecting a great deep tan Armani that would be perfect on you," Gertruda says hopefully.

"Can I wear those Armani earth tones?" I ask.

"It would be perfect for you," she repeats. She also says she would love to "furnish" any of my husband's needs. To my surprise (but why should

I be surprised?), personal shoppers are just as available to men as they are to women. Gertruda sends me the Armani by UPS, but the color is wrong for my no-makeup look. (Such items may be sent on approval, but you're charged for them nonetheless, and you have to go to the trouble of sending them back.)

I'm on my way to Macy's, my last stop on this coat safari. When I tell Sandy Richards, my personal shopper there, that I've never been to Macy's, she can't stop laughing. She takes me into the back room, where a few coats by Anne Klein and other designers have just arrived, but they are all too sporty for my needs. Sandy, a stylish, pretty young woman, speaks up. "You need more of a high-fashion coat. We will be getting in Valentino. We don't get Chanel. But if something comes in that I think you might like, I'll call you."

What's amazing is that I have felt no high pressure in the last two days. The only problem is my own regret that I can't buy a coat from every one of them. But the service really did help. By spending less than an hour in each of the six stores, I know exactly what coats are available.

Now I have to make up my mind. Trying on the orange Lacroix this morning made me realize that the hot pink is great-looking, but it's a secondary coat, a coat for someone who already owns her primary one and probably a dozen others. I live in a small New York apartment, and I don't have room for more than one winter coat. So where does that leave me? I think black and run back to Bendel's to try on the black Lagerfeld. Somehow it just doesn't do what I expect it to do. I guess I'm waiting for that feeling my mother always told me

I'd have when I met the right man. I can't get the spotted cat out of my head. I dash across the street to Judith at Bergdorf's. This time she takes me into a large, deliciously cool dressing room. She returns with the fake spotted-cat coat. It's better than I remembered. She's found out who made it, too, Anna Mucci, exclusively for Bergdorf's. "Try it on," she says, helping me into it. She stands back, smiling, watching me. I know it's right, and she does too. "It's high fashion *and* a real snow bunny," she says.

"I'll take it."

November 1990

Diamonds

If you've got it, don't flaunt it. That seems to be the slogan of the nineties so far, give or take a few pockets of stubbornly conspicuous consumption. Greed is no longer good, and the trappings of wealth, like the skins of wild animals, evoke scorn in the streets. We've all read about "dressing down" in *Vogue* and a lot of other places, haven't we? The new poverty, however, seems to have had no effect on the demand for that formidable rock of ages—the diamond.

Diamond sales are healthier than ever. Americans spent almost $12 billion on jewelry last year, a third more than they spent on all beauty products. At Tiffany's, diamond-engagement-ring sales rose 40 percent in 1992, on top of the previous year's 30 percent increase. Cartier is expanding the engagement-ring sections in all its stores. Diamond necklaces, ear studs, pendants, and such newfangled items as the "tennis bracelet" are selling briskly, and men's diamond engagement rings (ugh) have been coming on strong. Although

Tiffany's refuses to sell diamond-solitaire rings to men, because the store's design director, John Loring, thinks they're vulgar, such rings now account for 21 percent of all diamond-engagement-ring sales nationally.

As far as the big stones go, Sotheby's had one of its most successful jewelry auctions of the decade in Geneva last May; among the highlights was an 11.47-carat pear-shaped blue diamond that went for $3,643,793, an astonishing $317,680 a carat. "There are still enough people who want to wear that big diamond engagement ring," says John Block, Sotheby's jewelry expert and senior vice president. "But people are certainly more cautious these days. Instead of just wearing big diamonds flagrantly, they have a limousine and a driver take them to the vault on the way to the party, and then back to the vault on the way home."

How to explain the persistence of diamonds? The unbeatably romantic diamond mystique, for one thing, helped along by millions and millions of dollars a year spent in advertising and marketing. Ever since the fifteenth century, diamond rings have symbolized love and marriage. At first the custom applied only to kings and queens, but by the nineteenth century it had spread to the prosperous upper classes, and today 70 percent of American brides get that diamond ring. (I'm in the 30 percent that didn't; I got a yellow sapphire.) "It's an obligation, a tribal rite," says a recently remarried octogenarian I know. Julia Roberts got a big solitaire; Kim Basinger sports one too, and so does supermodel Iman.

Engagement rings are the meat and potatoes of the diamond business—they account for nearly a quarter of all diamond sales. The increased demands at Tiffany's and Cartier reflect the fact that marriages—or remarriages—are on the rise, perhaps in light of the new morality and the fear of AIDS. But De Beers, which controls more than 80 percent of the international diamond market and spends about $54 million a year to advertise and promote the sale of diamond jewelry, is not leaving anything to chance. De Beers's longtime advertising agency, NW Ayer, has been reminding couples since 1947 that "diamonds are forever," and suggests that the prospective husband should spend two months' salary on the ring—a rather heavy commitment. What helps to make diamonds "forever" is that they're the hardest substance known to man—marriage is hard too, but that doesn't seem to be the symbolism that NW Ayer has in mind. Recently the agency mounted a strenuous campaign to persuade husbands to buy their wives tenth-anniversary diamond bands, twenty-fifth-anniversary diamond necklaces, and other sparklers to celebrate the heroic achievement of staying married. NW Ayer is decidedly not promoting the "divorce necklace," an innovation that involves deconstructing the engagement ring and wearing the diamond as a pendant.

Love and marriage aside, diamonds are popping up in all sorts of new settings. Chanel has just come out with its first collection of diamond jewelry, featuring such novelties as a claspless, star-shaped necklace with its own cometlike trail. Inevitably, in the year of *Jurassic Park*, a young designer named Lori Gyl Mahler recently won NW Ayer's annual Art of Diamonds competition with a $7,000 diamond brooch in the shape of a stegosaurus. You can get your initials in diamonds from Fior-Drissage, to be worn as a pendant, at $3,500 per letter (one is enough, thank you); you can also get little diamond-studded crosses for $700 (M + J Savitt); and, if you want to be really in, you can always go down to Tourneau and get a diamond-sprinkled face for your gold Rolex. "We're seeing a trend now," says Cartier's president and CEO, Simon Critchell, "where people want watches that have a little diamond treatment. We do watches with diamond dials, bezels, cases, or bracelets. Diamonds are very attractive when they're done in a less obvious way, and people feel quite happy wearing them in the daytime."

Casual is a key word. Donna Karan has been talking about "diamonds and denim." Come to think of it, the idea of wearing a 30-carat, D flawless, emerald-cut diamond ring with blue jeans is something I could really relate to, at least in fantasy. I tried on a few like that at Cartier and at Harry Winston's when I was researching this piece. I looked at but didn't try on Harry Winston's Edwardian diamond-studded platinum dog collar, a far from casual item that Winston's Laurence Krashes says he can't keep in stock. "It has a sneeze clasp in back," Krashes says, "so that when the lady sneezes or sips champagne or swallows caviar, it gives a little." The cost was $1.5 million, I'm allergic to caviar, and my bank account doesn't have that kind of give.

Janis Savitt, one of the more with-it jewelry designers, has come out with a necklace of many black leather cords with individual diamonds hanging from them at irregular intervals—about 20 carats in all—selling for $475,000. This is a classic example of spending a fortune to achieve the casual look—throwaway chic. "You can mix things," says Savitt. "Wear your diamonds with silver, with copper, with wood, or with gold that's not too flashy." Flash is definitely out, which seems a little odd, since the primary function of a cut diamond is to refract light and send it back in a chromatic dazzle. Barry Kieselstein-Cord, another innovative jewelry designer, has done an eighteen-carat-gold cross studded with diamonds on one side, but you're supposed to wear the diamond side turned toward you, so that only you will know. Very nineties. Kieselstein-Cord was amazed that an Armenian like me, descended from a trading culture, from a long history of portable wealth, had no diamond jewelry. "Shame on you not knowing your heritage," he scolded. But in fact, Kieselstein-Cord himself feels that diamonds are just a teensy bit common. "It's a fabulous middle-class statement for someone who's saved the money," he told me. "For me, rubies come first."

Diamond beads threaded as a necklace may be the ultimate in casual chic. Fred Leighton, who specializes in antique and estate jewelry, has one made out of old Indian round diamonds strung on platinum wire, with nine very rare diamond briolettes hanging down from it like teardrops. "Old pieces set in silver and gold have a different sparkle from those big flashy clusters of diamonds that were popular in the eighties," says Mara Leighton, the head man's daughter. "Nineteenth-century stones were cut to catch the candlelight, so it's a much softer sparkle, as opposed to cuts like the modern 'radiant' [shaped like a square and faceted like a round], which is engineered to send off the biggest and brightest flash." Ward Landrigan, owner of the exclusive Verdura, agrees. "Right now the old-money look is in," he told me. "When I was head of jewelry at Sotheby's in the sixties, the big favorites were pear shapes and marquise cuts, which tend to give you more show per carat. Now the better older cuts are coming back—the emerald cut, the pillow-shaped cushion cut, which is the oldest cut of all—because it looks like you've had it longer."

Definitely out is parure, the Georgette Mosbacher look of matched jewelry ensembles. "Sets like that hark back to Napoleonic times," says Landrigan. "You'd have matching bracelets, rings, a brooch, earrings, tiara, necklace; you'd be totally decked out. The problem with that is you looked like you were on your way home from the jewelry store. For today's look, I think a great pair of earrings with a brooch is enough." There is no end of great earrings and brooches at Verdura, which is sort of a clubhouse for Mercedes Bass, Brooke Astor, Pamela Harriman, and other superchic jewel horses. Verdura himself made his name in the 1920s by designing new settings for the fabulous jewels that Coco Chanel picked up from her lover, the Duke of Westminster.

NW Ayer is actually promoting affordable parure with what it calls the diamond wardrobe. It's small-scale diamonds for the working girl—you can get a whole "classic" look with diamond ear studs, a pendant, the engagement ring, and the ubiquitous tennis bracelet. The tennis bracelet got its name from one that Chris Evert supposedly dropped on the center court at the U.S. Open a decade ago, and today it sells like U.S. Open

T-shirts. Depending on the size and quality of the stones, they cost anywhere from $1,000 to $20,000 (at Fortunoff) and are one of the most popular items to come along since Elsa Peretti democratized the diamond in 1974 with her (relatively) affordable Diamonds by the Yard.

What about the big stones, the spectacular, multicarat diamonds that have always excited the passions of queens and movie stars? They're still being bought and worn, but not in public—at least not in this country, where the fear of crime and the cost of insurance have reinforced the new austerity. Dowagers and trophy wives are acutely aware of what happened to Mrs. Marvin Davis, who flaunted her diamonds too fearlessly and was relieved of $10 million worth of them at gunpoint on the French Riviera this past spring. "After all, we're not living in the Stone Age," says Karl Lagerfeld, who wants it to be known that he has nothing to do with Chanel's new line of diamond jewelry. "Today they're not for display, unless it's a big stone on very young skin." At private dinner parties in New York, Los Angeles, and Palm Beach, you still see big diamond solitaires of fifteen carats and more, but the wearers usually turn them around when they leave so that only the band shows, and they almost never wear them to restaurants. *New York Post* columnist William Norwich told me that at a Saturday morning aerobics class he takes in a Southampton swimming pool, "Everyone's got a big clunker on." It's also quite okay to wear your rocks to work in the garden. When Calvin Klein bought his wife, Kelly, the former Duchess of Windsor's diamond ring at auction, she happily decided that the Duchess had gardened with it on because it was so scratched. Sharon Stone and Hillary Rodham Clinton made the ultimate statements about how to wear diamonds in this dress-down era. Stone appeared on the *Good Morning America* show in nothing but a white terry bathrobe and a diamond necklace, leading everyone to believe that she sleeps with her rocks. Clinton wore a diamond in the rough to her husband's inauguration; the uncut and unpolished 4.25-carat canary yellow diamond was found at Crater of Diamonds State Park near Murfreesboro, Arkansas, where for $4 you can go and dig up your own diamonds.

There's an old saying among diamond dealers that "the bigger the stone, the newer the money." And the fact is that these days the biggest and most spectacular stones are being sold to new customers in the Middle East and the Far East. Sheikh Ahmed Hassan Fitaihy, who owns a string of department stores in Saudi Arabia, has been buying at auction like a man possessed. "In the past three years he's bought 25 to 30 percent of every jewelry auction in New York, Geneva, and St. Moritz," says Guido Giovannini-Torelli, the editor of the trade newsletter *Diamond Insight*. The sheikh buys the biggest stones, which he names on the spot: the Jeddah Bride, the Star of the Desert. (If you buy a stone over 50 carats, you're supposed to name it.) "They're all pear shaped," says Giovannni-Torelli. "The pear shape is very popular in Saudi Arabia." According to Michael Kazanjian, one of the leading jewelers on the West Coast (no relation to the author, worse luck), the American trend of dressing down has not caught on in Saudi Arabia. "There they like sets and ornate jewelry, a complete ensemble of bracelet, earrings, necklace, and a ring." In the Far East—Japan, Singapore, Hong Kong—the tendency is "to buy very simple things," Kazanjian says. "As opposed to Americans, who buy a lot of designed pieces of jewelry, the Orientals are more concerned about the quality of the stones." Pear-shaped diamonds sell poorly in the Far East, though, according to Ward Landrigan, "because they say the diamonds are in the form of tears, and you don't buy sadness."

The development of the Middle and Far Eastern markets has been one of the recent triumphs of the diamond syndicate's marketing strategy, and it has largely offset any defections by American and European customers. In Japan, where only 6 percent of the brides wore diamond engagement rings in 1966, the figure now, thanks to NW Ayer's relentless promotion, is 76 percent. Crown Princess Masako received a three-carat, D flawless solitaire from Crown Prince Naruhito last spring before their marriage, but she doesn't wear it in public because it is a "personal treasure."

Are diamonds still a girl's best friend? They never were, if the girl was thinking investment. The retail markup makes it highly unlikely that most diamonds will ever be worth more than the buyer paid for them. "We don't sell diamonds for investments," Harry Winston's veteran expert Laurence Krashes told me emphatically. Every other reputable jeweler says the same thing. Rampant speculation in the late seventies and early eighties drove diamond prices to a record $63,000 per carat for the highest quality (D flawless) diamond, and when the market broke in 1982 a lot of speculators got burned. The famous Taylor-Burton diamond, which Richard Burton bought for Elizabeth Taylor in 1969 for $1.1 million, was put up for sale a decade later at $4 million; after languishing for quite a while on the market, it was finally sold to a dealer for slightly more than $2 million, but with inflation and insurance costs, that actually added up to a loss for Liz.

These days a really savvy mistress should probably hold out for one of the fancy pink or blue diamonds that are currently bringing the highest prices on the market, or for the immense D color "potentially" flawless, such as the 78.54-carat Archduke Joseph diamond that is up for sale at Christie's in Geneva on November 18. Our savvy mistress will obviously know the Four C's of diamond buying—carat, cut, color, and clarity—but the rest of you, now, pay attention. Carat means weight (one carat = 200 milligrams). Cut has to do with the way a stone is faceted to gather and throw back the light. Clarity refers to the absence of the microscopic blemishes called inclusions; no diamond is perfect, but one rated Fl is as flawless as you can get, and anything lower than VS_2 (Very Slight $Inclusions_2$) is not a good buy. Got that? Color in diamonds is rated on a scale from D, which is colorless, down to Z; as the scale descends, the diamond gets yellower and less valuable—unless you go beyond Z all the way to Fancy Intense Yellow, which is very rare and very valuable. Sotheby's is selling the largest Fancy Intense Yellow ever certified by the Gemological Institute of America at its auction in Geneva this November. It's nearly 60 carats, and the estimate is about $1.5 million. "But listen," says Guido Giovannini-Torelli, "unless it's a very, very big, intense stone, forget about the yellows. There are many, many of them. But to see a pink or a blue, this is rare. Only the very, very rich and the very, very refined people have them. This is a real statement. And there's something better than that: the red diamond. There are only six in the world, and they cost a million a carat. One was sold at Christie's in 1987, reportedly to the Sultan of Brunei." (Savvy mistress, take note.)

Contrary to popular belief, there is no shortage of small, less-than-flawless diamonds. They are now being mined in 20 countries, and De Beers's success in controlling their production and distribution—and thus maintaining prices—is one of the marvels of the age. (It is also the subject of Stefan Kanfer's new book, *The Last Empire* [Farrar, Straus & Giroux].) Antitrust laws prevent De Beers from operating openly in the United States, but so far the syndicate has beaten back or absorbed every challenge, including the constant threat of scientifically produced diamonds for industrial uses. Synthetics have the same problem as zircons—they can never compete with the emotionally based appeal of the real thing.

"Diamonds continue to be the ultimate symbol of love," as Lynn Ramsey of NW Ayer's Diamond Information Center glowingly puts it. "Nothing else even comes close." Diamond promoters were uniformly scandalized when Prince Charles gave Lady Di a sapphire engagement ring. (Something like mine, I guess, only a trifle larger.) "But look what happened to her," says Lynn Ramsey. "She should have gotten a diamond."

November 1993

the
armani
jacket

The need to own an Armani jacket stole over me gradually, so gradually that by the time I became fully aware of it, I already wanted one quite a lot. I hardly ever buy top-of-the-line designer clothes—the last time I had the urge was four years ago, when I went all out and got my first Chanel suit. The Armani jacket seems to have edged out the Chanel suit as this decade's ultimate piece of clothing. A lot of women I know are addicted to its fluid, understated, soft, versatile, and blissfully comfortable style, and a lot of famous women I don't know have been photographed wearing it: Diane Sawyer, Michelle Pfeiffer, Anjelica Huston, Winona Ryder, Jodie Foster, Ali MacGraw, Lauren Bacall, Sherry Lansing, Gayfryd Steinberg. (Not Hillary Rodham Clinton, though, and definitely not Ivana Trump.) Richard Gere and Cindy Crawford wore complementary Armani suits to their wedding in 1991. Annette Bening and Maria Shriver got through their pregnancies in Armani jackets. The Armani jacket has become the antidote to all the 1980s flashy, aggressive power dressing that we now despise. It's the status symbol that doesn't declare itself, conferring status without symbol. How can I resist?

What I want, specifically, is one of the jackets from the Armani spring collection that previewed in Milan last fall. There are five stores in New York where you can buy Armani's signature Borgonuovo collection, or "black label" line: Bloomingdale's, Saks Fifth Avenue, Bergdorf Goodman, Barney's New York, and the flagship Armani store on Madison Avenue. I start with Bloomingdale's. Nobody seems to want to pay any attention to me at Bloomingdale's Armani boutique, which I visit in early December. Maybe, in my Banana Republic jeans and ten-year-old Yves Saint Laurent jacket, I don't measure up as an Armani type. My friend Brooke says Armani is too big for me anyway. "He designs for big, tall women," she says. That's been one of my worries, and so has the price; Armani's black-label jackets go for something like $1,300. There's also Le Collezioni, with less costly fabrics, where a jacket retails for $800 to $900, and Emporio Armani, a whole different line of cuts and fabrics for younger bodies, at half that much.

When a saleswoman finally deigns to approach me, and I ask if I can see the book for the spring collection, the answer is no. The spring book isn't in yet. In any case, they've already ordered what they'll be showing from the book. Would I like to be invited to their trunk show in February? She takes my name and says she'll call. Before leaving, I try on one of the winter jackets that are on view, just to get the feel of it. It feels wonderful, but the size—38—is way too big for me. Could I try a smaller size? "It doesn't come any smaller," she says. "You just need a pinch here in the back, take in the shoulders a bit, take in the waist, and lift the sleeves." That's all? Feeling a trifle deflated, I move on.

It is more or less the same story at the other department stores. No spring book yet. They'll invite me to the trunk show, but there's no assurance I can get the jacket I want. Saks won't even take my name—the saleswoman says I should call her because she "might forget." Some stores are more gracious than others. At Bergdorf's, a personal shopper unexpectedly greets me at the door, takes me to Armani, and promises she'll get me in the day before the trunk show opens. At Barney's new palace on Madison and Sixty-first, a saleswoman informs me that they do carry my size, 36. (The other department stores had insisted that 38 was the smallest; what would the well-known perfectionist Giorgio Armani have to say about that?) The saleswoman also trots me over to the nearby boutique of Jil Sander, whose designs have a lot in common with Armani's; I like them, but the Armani mystique has me enthralled.

At the Armani store, nobody seems to notice me even though I'm the only shopper on the floor. I stand conspicuously near a saleswoman who seems to be having an interminable conversation on the telephone. Finally, another one comes rushing by and I do my best to tackle her. "Check in early February," she calls back over her shoulder. No hard sell here.

While waiting it out, I decide to do a little research. Giorgio Armani has been making women's jackets since 1975, a year after he burst on the scene as a designer of men's clothes. "I was amazed when I saw women friends wanting to wear the jackets I made for men," Armani said in his voice-over commentary for the half-hour film Martin Scorsese made about him in 1990. (Scorsese is an old friend of Armani's; he wears his jackets all the time.) "They liked plain, soft, flowing jackets they could move in freely and naturally, like a second skin." The film, whose script was written by *The Age of Innocence* screenwriter Jay Cocks and which had its U.S. premiere at the Museum of Modern Art, is an act of canonization as well as an ode to the jacket. "I created all my work around the jacket," said Saint Giorgio. "It was my point of departure for everything. . . . My small but crucial discovery was making jackets that fall in an unexpected natural way. I tried new techniques, like removing the padding and the interlining. . . . I altered the way jackets were buttoned and radically modified the proportions. What used to be considered a defect became the basis for a new shape—a new jacket." In the process, he developed a jacket that was as light and as comfortable as a shirt, sensual but not very sexy, and right for any occasion. Although intricately constructed and beautifully made, Armani's jackets have a "deconstructed," minimalist look, free of signature buttons or self-congratulatory logos, that fits right in with the zeitgeist. He was the first postmodern fashion designer, doing for the jacket what others were doing for philosophy, architecture, and art.

Some people collect Armani jackets like paintings. Writer Joan Juliet Buck, a *femme du monde* if ever there was one, has at least twenty of them. She buys two a season when she's feeling rich enough. "If you divide the cost per wear, they cost about three cents," she says. "Armani jackets age differently from other clothes. Other jackets go seriously out of style. Old Armani jackets just get exhausted from overuse—they droop. It's really about simplifying your life. You reach a certain age, get past forty, you know who you are, and you know what looks good on you. You think of getting through life elegantly with behavior that's not going to drive other people crazy. I think Armani reflects that."

Professional women (aren't we all these days?) love the practicality of the Armani jacket. It goes with almost anything—Armani or not—and it's so comfortable that you forget you're wearing it. I keep hearing women say that you're "taken seriously" when you wear one. "If you go into a boardroom in a canary yellow suit and a very short skirt, it's hard to be taken seriously," one corporate superstar tells me—she is wearing a beige wool crepe Armani jacket over matching wide-legged pants. But you don't have to match to be taken seriously. The Armani jacket alone carries the seriousness of the suit.

When Ali MacGraw's Malibu house burned to the ground last November, one of the things she really missed was her twelve-year-old Armani tuxedo jacket. "I long ago stopped wearing the pants, but the jacket I wore all the time," she tells me. "It was one of the most beautifully fitting and beautifully cut pieces of clothing I've ever owned. Year after year after year, I traveled in it. The fabric was amazing, the workmanship was amazing. The cut was wonderful on my big-boned carcass."

She went right out after the fire and got herself a black wool crepe Armani jacket. MacGraw thinks it's interesting that Armani has become such a hit in Los Angeles. (The Armani boutique on Rodeo Drive opened in 1988.) "Los Angeles is traditionally the land of no taste, and along came this megasweep of Armani to teach all those ladies how to dress," she says. Agents, studio executives, and other high-powered Hollywood women are now "wearing a uniform that makes them look better than they ever looked. Of course, I think some people look better in it than others. A curvaceous body—the serious, old-fashioned movie star body—is less terrific in it than a more athletic shape. It looks ludicrous with stiletto heels, nail polish, tons of jewelry and makeup. You have to know how to wear it."

Anjelica Huston, a good Armani jacketeer, knows just how to wear it, and she tends to wear a lot of black and white and red. A year and a half ago, she got married in a "diamond white" Armani jacket over a white Armani dress. "He's simple," she has said of Armani, "which is the hardest thing in the world."

Like all the great classic icons of fashion—the Chanel suit, the Kelly bag, the Manolo Blahnik pump—the Armani jacket is widely copied. Many of the top American designers have appropriated the tapered, stripped-down Armani look and the subtle Armani color palette in their own jackets. None of this has had much effect on demand for the real thing. Sales of Armani black-label jackets, which are made in a small factory outside Milan that has been run by the same family for several generations, have been increasing by 15 to 20 percent a year over the last three or four years. American women bought just under 30,000 of them last year. (American men bought a third that many for themselves; does this mean that women care more about being taken seriously?) Because the style changes from year to year are subtle rather than drastic, and because the things wear so well, there's an Armani army out there that never wears anything else.

Okay, so what about my spring jacket? It's been more than a month since I hit the stores, and nobody has called me about coming in. (Nobody ever does call me, as it turns out.) I call the Armani store, and a friendly (surprise!) saleswoman named Jenny tells me to come on over, they've got the spring book, and a few jackets have already arrived. Come early in the morning, she says, when it's not crowded. I get there at ten o'clock on the dot the next morning. The book is about four inches thick and somewhat overwhelming. I see shawl-collared jackets, collarless jackets, cardigan-style jackets, asymmetrical jackets, and of course the classic Armani blazers, both single-and double-breasted, with notched or peaked lapels. There's a "cobra jacket" that buttons at the neck with a banded collar. Jackets with loops instead of buttonholes; jackets with only one button, perfectly placed; jackets that are bordered with a fine cord that runs down the front and ties at the waist. Linen jackets, wool crepe jackets, cotton jackets, silk jackets. A sea of muted earth-colored fabrics—beige, gray, taupe, stone, sand, jellyfish, navy, black, white. Jackets, jackets, jackets. I can't cope with shopping from the book. I try on several of the newly arrived spring jackets, all of which seem to be available in size 36; the salesman says that more are arriving every day. Armani's spring jackets come in sixteen styles, each of which can be had in a bewildering variety of lusciously discreet fabrics and discreet colors. The problem isn't finding a jacket, it's making a decision. I beat a strategic retreat.

My pal Brooke, one of the great shoppers, comes with me the next day. The friendly Jenny helps me this time; she turns out to be just my height, and she looks cool in Armani's navy wool crepe pantsuit. Brooke is all authority. She spurns the three jackets that I had put on hold and pulls out several others I would never have thought of trying—a textured cotton-and-silk number with a mandarin collar; a collarless one in stone-colored wool crepe; and a tapered white linen jacket with a slim rounded lapel and a single button that closes with a loop. They're all very long, and Brooke likes each one. "See, you're not too small for Armani," she says, as if it hadn't been her idea that I was. The truth is, they all make me feel taller. They make me feel wonderful, in fact; there's a degree of unconfined comfort that I've never had in a jacket before. We narrow it down to the collarless wool crepe and the one-button linen. I go back and forth between them, slipping into one and then the other. I'm leaning toward the one-button, but I'd rather have it in another fabric—the stone wool crepe, specifically. Jenny brings out the swatch book and turns to that jacket. No dice. It doesn't come in wool crepe. It does come in a loosely woven pale beige linen blend along with eight other fabric choices. After another twenty minutes of agonizing over colors and materials, I pick the beige linen.

A month later, it's mine. The pleasure it gives me is amazing. This featherlight, minimal *wisp* of a jacket immediately registers as one of my all-time favorite pieces of clothing. It's instant style—something I can wear anywhere and everywhere without even thinking about it. The Armani secret is all in the cut and the fabric. My jacket hangs from the shoulder in a smooth glide, skimming my body like a caress. It's true, what they say: The feeling is sensual rather than sexual. It looks great with jeans, which is how I'll mostly wear it, and it looks just as good with my black pleated skirt and a T-shirt. But wait a minute. I can't get into the pockets! Two side pockets are clearly visible when I turn the jacket inside out and hold it up to the light, but there's no mere tacking stitch here—it's absolutely impossible to get in them. Pockets have always been important to me—that was one of the things I wanted in a jacket—but I can see that the slightest bulge would wreak havoc on Armani's sinuous line. Oh, well, I'll adapt. As Ali MacGraw says, you have to know how to wear an Armani. And I can see I'm never going to want to take this one off.

In fact, I wear it onto the airplane the morning it arrives. My husband and I are going to visit his married daughter in Los Angeles. Driving from the airport in her Ford Explorer, I get the once-over from Sherrick, her precocious seven-year-old. "Why do you have only one button?" he asks. "Did you lose the other two?"

"No," I explain. "That's how it comes. Don't you like it?"

Pause for further scrutiny. "It's okay," he says, with his most winning smile.

May 1994

the boot

The word has come down from Mount Olympus, the message has gone out: This is the year of the boot. At the fall collections in Paris, Milan, and New York, there was hardly a shoe to be seen. Karl Lagerfeld sent his Chanel models out in moon boots swathed in monkey fur and gold chains, in crotch-high leather riding boots, in belle epoque pointy-toed granny lace-ups. Jean Paul Gaultier equipped his shock troops with heavy-duty black velvet engineer boots with inch-thick lugged soles. Donna Karan, Ralph Lauren, and the generalissimos of American fashion—even Bill Blass—put every puss in boots. Calvin Klein now says he's planning a show of underwear with boots (whatever that implies). There's no getting around it, boots are everywhere.

And once again, this fashion laggard is struggling to catch up. Except for my one pair of well-scuffed green suede Tony Lama cowboy boots, I've never gone in for the things. I don't even own a pair of galoshes, much to my husband's disgust, so

I tend to stay inside when it snows. In the past three weeks, though, I've looked at hundreds of boots, talked with designers, and tried on samples until my toes ached. And I'm convinced. There's a boot for everybody out there, maybe more than one for me. There are so many alternatives and so many choices, in fact, that you can even avoid the feeling that you're being dictated to once again by the generalissimos. Boots are an idea whose time has definitely come back.

The first question, I guess, is, Why? And the obvious answer is simply that they've been away for so long. Not since Courrèges's little white plastic boots in the sixties has there been a real focus on female bootery, and that's a long time in the fashion cycle. (There were some early sightings in *Vogue* last summer, but now there's a full-fledged invasion.) The more immediate reason, however, is that boots seem to be the ideal complement to the new ultrafeminine, gossamer, flyaway clothes. Boots go wonderfully with long skirts, short A-line skirts, or with no skirts at all—high over-the-knee boots worn with leggings and topped with a long jacket. "I think it is the only footwear to go with the proportions of the moment," Karl Lagerfeld told me. "They look very good with the soft, floating clothes and with the way pants, dresses, and skirts are shaped right now. I love the musketeer look of a woman wearing tights, a long flared jacket, and those high boots with small heels—it's a very beautiful and sexy look."

Calvin Klein, who is heavily into black-leather spat-type ankle boots, says that the "strong foot" is the thing this season. "It's not about being delicate right now, it's about being tough and strong and hard. It's more about leather than it is about suede. And boots just look great with soft, pretty dresses. This is not a military thing. The boot has that feeling, of course, but it's used in such a whole other way that it grounds the foot, and then everything else is as light as air."

Most fashion trends have some input from the street these days, and this one is no exception. What really triggered the boot brigade were the grunge dressers in Seattle and their abominable Doc Martens a couple of seasons back. The streets have been filled with kids in thick-soled clodhoppers ever since. Now the designers, bless their trendy hearts, have adapted this improbable style and turned it into clunky chic. In addition to Gaultier's black velvet engineer boot, we have Calvin Klein's distressed-leather combat boot, Ralph Lauren's stacked-heel work boot, and spirited variations by Nathalie Marciano for Guess and just about every other hot designer. (The clodhopper style has even invaded New York City bus shelters, where a public service ad shows just such an item and urges citizens to GIVE RACISM THE BOOT.)

Sam & Libby's Cross Country ($85), a Doc Marten knockoff if ever I've seen one, "is a logger boot from Amsterdam," I was told by Beth Ann Orchulli, Sam's assistant. When I asked how it differs from a Doc Marten, she said it has "heavier heels and a sturdier wood-inlay sole." And how do we fit such clunkers into our new wardrobe? Beats me. I don't do much logging, and I hate the way they look.

Clunky chic is only a small part of what's going on, though. There are granny boots of all kinds, long and short, laced front and back, trussed and dressed with rhinestones or other baubles, most of them with fiendishly pointed toes. Knee-high riding boots are everywhere, in everything from Fendi's $550 patchwork four-color ostrich to Prada's sumptuous grommeted leather to Chanel's exquisite versions in velvet, nuBuck, and suede ($900). Over-the-knee boots in soft leather, suede, Lycra, and more exotic materials—Andrea Pfister has one in gold brocade tapestry fabric for $800—are terrific for women with the thighs to carry them off. (I'm not one of them. My campaign with a personal thigh trainer lapsed a year ago.)

There are ankle boots and wedge boots and biker boots and spat boots. Patrick Cox offers a pink fur-topped half-calf, and Prada's black Mongolian-lamb job looks just like an excited poodle. Chanel's moon boot with monkey fur is a dead ringer for the après-ski fashion of the seventies.

But what am I to do? My rule of foot is, when in doubt, call Manolo. "I've been doing boots for years, but this year I've done three times as many," Manolo Blahnik tells me from his house in the Canary Islands. "I'm doing boots in velvets, in brocades, in the most extravagant materials." (The grunge look has never ruffled Manolo's imagination.) "It's unabashedly feminine this year and sexy at the same time. Don't you think so? I have to keep doing things like that, even if people are just wanting more and more horrible cowboy boots." So much for my Tony Lamas.

"The best boot of all time," Manolo goes on to say, "was the square-toed satin boot, kind of 1851 French—*that* was the most beautiful. There is one copy at the Musée Carnavalet. How can they top that thing? In fact, Courrèges inspired himself by that." This year, Manolo inspired himself by "the wonderful Empress Eugenie, consort of Napoleon III. She always wore the most beautiful velvet-and-satin boot. That is the feeling that I have this year."

The feeling I have is that Manolo raises feet to new heights—his boots and shoes are more like jewelry than footgear. I'd like to have all of his boots. There's Maka ($625), the black suede above-the-ankle Victorian boot with buttons up the side (they snap, so you don't have to bother with the buttons), and Clinta ($495), a kid ankle boot with Manolo's new bobbin heel ("bobeen hill" in Manolo-speak) that is elasticized at the sides so you can slip right into it. He named this one for Chelsea Clinton, because it's like a Chelsea boot. Bona ($825), a calf-hugging suede boot with a little chunky Cuban heel that you can wear over the knee or fold down, zips up the back. It's a perfect boot. "I *love* the idea of z-z-zip, and you take it off," Manolo tells me. "Oh, goodness gracious, the revealing. The idea of taking it off, like a glove, is a very sexual sense of gesture. Taking a boot off the leg is beautiful."

Pedia ($750) is the quintessential romantic boot, done in two velvets—black on the bottom and indigo on top, tied with satin lace on the side. Bottina ($430) is Manolo's idea of a granny boot. It laces up the front, but more important, it's built on top of his Sophia Loren clog. He did this one for Isaac Mizrahi.

I ask Manolo if there is a woman who can't wear a boot. "I don't think so. Even ladies with awful legs, like huge columns, they get very masked by the boot. The best idea for covering up terrible mistakes of nature is the boot."

When I go to the showrooms to try on some of the new boots, the problem is too many options, not too few. My first stop is at Sam & Libby, a company that specializes in "fashion forward" styles in affordably priced synthetic materials—from $35 on up. Its Just Libby line, which uses real leather, is slightly more sophisticated and slightly more expensive. The whole panoply of new styles is here, with special emphasis on the combat mode in black. Clomping around in lugged soles and five-inch heels with platforms makes me feel a little like Wonder Woman, but something tells me that Wonder Woman is more than I want to take on just now.

At Ralph Lauren, boots are arranged on a partner's desk, in a cozy room with an Oriental carpet. The smell of expensive leather and skillful marketing is in the air. Ralph Lauren has done boots since day one, but this season he's come up with a host of new ones that carry overtones of romantic militarism and echoes of Old Russia. I try on his Cossack boot ($575), a riding boot that turned out to be too high for me. The Alexandra ($595), a granny boot that comes just above the ankle, is wonderfully comfortable (like all Lauren's boots), but I decide that granny boots are not for me—even with speed hooks, the lacing and the unlacing is too labor intensive. I love his Biker Boot ($275) in black leather with a lugged sole, a bit of a heel, and a zipper in back, but my favorite is the Stratton ($225)—suavely raked and just to the ankle, it is modeled after the cross-country ski boot.

I also investigate Guess, Calvin Klein, Anne Klein, Yves Saint Laurent, Chanel, Diego Della Valle, and Prada. Every one of them has a full range of boots, although Saint Laurent and Anne Klein tend to steer clear of the macho influence. At Diego Della Valle, shoemaker to the stars, I try on a navy blue satin flat boot with speed laces and a big rhinestone in back. Sharon Stone wears this in *Sliver,* I am told. In fact, Sharon Stone buys most of her shoes here. (Other customers include Barbra Streisand, Geena Davis, Richard Gere, Elizabeth Taylor, and Arnold Schwarzenegger.) The boots are fantastic, but I'm no more Sharon Stone than I am Wonder Woman.

Prada's black Mongolian lamb's-fur boot (the excited poodle) looks great too, but it's a big girl's boot; you need a lot of leg between where it leaves off and your jacket begins, and, at five-feet-two, I don't have it. When I asked Karl Lagerfeld what was the right boot for a small person, he had said, "You always ask this question because you're not the Eiffel Tower, but as long as the proportions are good, anything can work. You should wear a boot with heels, not too high on the leg, not too tight."

At Yves Saint Laurent, I'm crazy about a black suede, rubber soled, lace-up walking boot called Nepal ($145). It's just right for me. I can run around SoHo with it all fall and winter and never have sore feet. I decide a riding boot is a must, and one that particularly appeals to me is Chanel's Field Boot in black velvet. These boots are made for walking. They're comfortable, they're elegant, and they go with everything I own or could even dream of owning.

Don't think, by the way, that you can just go to H. Kauffman & Sons and buy your boots there; real riding boots, which cost anywhere from $145 to $350, are designed for the stirrup, not the street, and they're acutely uncomfortable to walk around in.

After three weeks of looking, though, I realize that the boot of the year for me is Manolo Blahnik's Gaucha ($590), a butter-soft, midcalf, flat boot with leather tie-ups on the side. This is his version of the traditional Argentinean cowboy's boot. Made of a wonderful rugged calf, it looks as if it would be the ideal successor to my Tony Lamas. It's as comfortable and eye-catching as my Manolo mules, and how can anything be better than that?

My husband insists I'm still going to need galoshes, but I'll find some way to put that off. Practicality is a last resort, after all. When I talked to Isaac Mizrahi, he said, "We don't need boots for the most part, do we? It's just this kind of romantic image. Unless you're going to war or plowing the fields, they're not particularly practical. Boots are just so good-looking. It's all about vanity."

So what else is new?

August 1993

thin thighs

One of my earliest memories is that I have plump thighs and my sister doesn't. Over the years, I've dieted conscientiously, exercised religiously, worn black tights whenever I could, and blamed my mother because I inherited her legs (my sister got my father's). Last July I told my sister, who is now a physician and who still has perfect legs, that I was thinking of going to a personal trainer to get rid of my fat thighs. "It won't work," she said. "But if it matters that much to you, why don't you have liposuction?"

What a word. I can't even bear to say it. No thanks.

As I dip a toe into my forties, I decide to hell with it. I'm going to try a personal trainer. It's an idea that's put me off until now because it sounded like 1980s self-indulgence. But nothing else has worked. I'll give it five months.

Before choosing my trainer, I shop around. I begin with a Manhattan trainer who works with clients at home. Kate Gyllenhaal, a professional dancer/choreographer who started Homebodies, comes to my apartment at eight o'clock one July morning. She asks me to put on a leotard so she can look me over—she means my thighs. Out comes the tape measure. What? The top of my thigh is twenty-one inches—as large as my waist? We do a brief workout. Kate's movements are gentle and seem to hit just the right spots, but during our session my phone rings five times. I can hear the messages as I squat into position. Maybe I don't want to work out at home.

"You'll see results in a month with Radu," Radu Teodorescu tells me when I visit his studio. Romanian-born Radu is known as the toughest trainer in New York. This bullet of a man—he's five feet six inches and weighs 158 pounds—trains Bianca Jagger, John F. Kennedy, Jr., Ellen Barkin, Calvin Klein, and many of the current supermodels. The studio is bare bones—no air-conditioning. Lots of heavy weights and a few weight machines. Not much else.

But who needs more when you've got Radu? I'm wearing a black shift to my knees. He pinches my arms, pulls at my calves, frisks me up and down. "Not bad," he says. Turning to a woman wearing black Lycra and pumping iron, he barks, "Go do chin-ups." He reminds me of a lion tamer. Back to me. "The pectoral muscle, I'd beef it up. The adductors, not bad."

The what? He points to a chart of the human body and indicates the thigh area just southeast of the buttocks. "It's the hardest part to reduce, especially for Italian and Jewish girls." This Armenian girl has the same problem, but lion tamers make her a little uneasy.

At the Sports Training Institute I look down onto a football-field-size room full of state-of-the-art workout equipment with not-so-state-of-the-art sweating and grunting bodies—mostly men's. It's like the second circle of hell. As I walk through the aisles between machinery and bodies with another potential trainer, the groans become louder and the sweat is heavier and I want to go home.

Before I do, I stop in to see Ann Piccirillo at Manhattan Body, where I've been taking classes for the last couple of years. I like the class, but it hasn't done anything for my thighs. I tell Ann my problem and ask if she can work with me privately. The answer is yes, and the price is sixty dollars an hour. A professional dancer before she started Manhattan Body, Ann has a lean, well-defined body and a down-to-earth way about her that I like. And her no-frills studio is only two blocks from my apartment. After a weekend of cogitation, these are the factors that stick in my mind. I choose Ann.

August 1: 1:00 P.M. My first session with Ann. "I'd like to make your legs long and lean, not just build muscles," she says. "Long, lean, and feminine. That's the kind of body I do here. If somebody wants bodybuilding, don't come to me." I like the sound of the word "long."

She looks me over, fore and aft in my black leotard. "You appear delicate. I don't want to build up your muscles too much. Bottom-heavy people like you, I tell them to eliminate three things from their diet. Number one is bread." I love Eli's sourdough bread, and I keep hearing that carbohydrates are at the top of everybody's healthy-eating list, but okay. What else?

"Butter and anything with fat, like peanut

butter, mayonnaise, nuts, red meat. And high-fat dairy products like cheeses and whole milk."

What's the third thing?

"Bubbles."

"Bubbles!?"

"Bubbles. Nothing carbonated."

"No Diet Coke? No Pellegrino? Why on earth not?"

"Absolutely no bubbles. Try it for a month."

Perplexingly enough, she can't explain the bubbles ban. She says she'll get an explanation for me, but meanwhile, just do as I'm told. Only one captain on this ship.

I tell Ann I'd also like to beef up my pectorals and eliminate any UADD (designer Michael Kors's term, meaning Under Arm Dingle Dangle). "We can do that."

"When do you think I'll start to see results?"

"By the end of the month."

We start right in. Some stretching, followed by weight lifting. She sits me on a chair and hands me a six-pound weight. In class, the most I've ever lifted is two pounds. She shows me how to work my biceps. Then my triceps. Next she wraps one-pound weights around my ankles.

"I'm going to work the top of your body with heavier weights because there's no fat there. And I'm going to use lighter weights and a lot of repetitions on the bottom. I want to slim your legs with diet first, and then we'll go to heavier weights."

Our first session lasts almost two hours. Ann doesn't weigh or measure me. "I believe in watching your body change and you seeing and feeling the results." But she does make sure I know my quads from my hamstrings and how to isolate each muscle to make it work to capacity. In all my years of taking exercise classes, I've never learned how to do this. We decide to meet three times a week to begin with.

I get through my first afternoon and night without a Diet Coke and pass on Eli's sourdough bread at dinner. And now, at my bedside, I've got a glass of Poland Spring water—flat—instead of my usual bubbly.

"How are you doing without your bubbles?" she asks at our next session. She still can't explain why, but she's determined to keep me bubble-free. Ann puts me through some new exercises that attack my quads, hamstrings, outer thighs, upper outer thighs (the Italian and Jewish part), inner thighs, and buttocks. She excels at figuring out different ways to torment the same muscles.

Before I leave, she gives me a wad of loose-leaf sheets with instructions for a one-hour workout I can do on my own. She also gives me a pair of four-inch-wide elasticized bands, one red and one green, that take the place of weights—you stretch them to work arm and leg muscles.

August 3: I'm developing quite a relationship with unadorned tuna fish—no mayonnaise. If I like, I can add some balsamic vinegar.

August 4: Away for the weekend. My first movie without Diet Coke. I've been exercising with the red and green bands, as directed. I'm also eating a lot of dry cereal—Müeslix without any milk. I still don't understand why the hell I can't have a Diet Coke.

August 6: Two o'clock workout. We start with thirty minutes of stepping, talking as we step "because it gets your heart going faster." Then Ann hands me the green rubber band, which is firmer than the red. After another half hour of stretching and pulling, I'm free to go.

The next day we do lots of stepping again, and everything seems harder. More than an hour later, I'm aching and exhausted. Ann gives me the name of a good masseuse. I hobble home and climb straight into a hot tub. No relief. Another hot bath two hours later and then to bed. Can I continue with this? My fat thighs don't look any different, and I crave a Diet Coke.

August 8: Struggling out of bed, my legs feel like they don't work. My whole body aches. I don't think I can make it to my eleven o'clock class. But I do. I'm dedicated to this. When Ann sees me totter in, she takes pity on me. No stepping today. This class lasts only an hour—thank God.

On Monday I meet with Ann again. We talk a lot, as usual. She tells me about her life—her husband, Nick, is six years younger than she is and hates to exercise. She tells me she thinks that my bottom heaviness is a product of my profession—sitting and writing. I should change professions? When we finish stepping, Ann says, "I'm going to bring in Nick's stationary bike." (She bought it for him, but he doesn't use it.) "I'm going to be thinking up new ways to torture your legs." Thanks a lot, Ann.

August 20: Nick's bike has appeared in the massage room. The bike has a screen that tells me how fast I'm riding and how many calories I'm burning off. But after twenty minutes on it, I've burned off only sixty calories.

Exercise continues at a furious pace throughout August. I keep to my diet except for the three chocolate diet cookies (twenty calories each) I eat on August 31. My red band snapped on August 29 on number twenty-one of my leg kicks, so I've been struggling with the firmer green band.

September 3: Ann is pleased with my biceps but not with my thighs. I fess up to the three diet cookies and to a roast beef sandwich I had on the way to today's class.

"Oh, my God."

"But I didn't eat the bread, and I had it without mayonnaise. Just salt." She announces that she's going to take away my salt and sugar.

She works me out—upper and lower body—for an hour, then condemns me to twenty minutes on the bike at level one and twelve more minutes at level two. I leave exhausted, and I can't tell if my legs are coming with me.

At our next session, Ann tells me that in order to achieve what we want with my fat legs, I have to ride the bike for fifty-two minutes every day until the end of the year. This is very depressing. Maybe I like my fat legs after all.

September 4: At 9:00 A.M., I ride the bike for thirty-four minutes—this is my little rebellion—at two different levels and burn off one hundred calories. That just about equals the orange juice (from one orange) I had this morning. I go back at one o'clock and work with Ann till two. At this rate, it's going to be hard to find time for anything but exercise. *Is it worth it?*

Throughout September, Ann tries to keep me to 850 bubble-free calories a day (even though she doesn't believe in counting calories and in the face of *The New York Times*'s report on how bad crash dieting is for us). I also bicycle fourteen nonexistent miles every day.

September 16: Early in the morning my husband says, "Your legs really have gotten thinner and more shapely." First sign that all this pain and denial is paying off.

September 18: After a thorough workout, and just before I leave for an overnight trip to Los Angeles, Ann tells me to cut back on pasta. "No more Parmesan. Pasta only two or three times a week." (I never use sauce on my pasta, only Parmesan. This is a serious blow.) "And cut out the orange juice." (I silently decide not to cut out the orange juice.)

September 20: A massage by Ko at the Beverly Wilshire. "You're too skinny," he tells me.

September 22: At dinner in New York, two friends say, "Don't lose any more weight."

September 23: Weight hasn't changed much. I'm down only two pounds on the scale, but fat is being replaced by muscle, which weighs more. Ann sees real changes in my legs for the first time. "The bike is working. The area around your knees has slimmed down. And your quads are looking good. Now we're ready to start with heavier leg weights."

September 25: Ann attaches a five-pound padded weight to my right ankle and a one-and-a-half pounder above that. She does the same to my left leg. After fifty grueling quad kicks and fifty hamstring curls with both legs, she gives me more leg homework.

September 26: I burn off two hundred calories on the bike. Tonight, a private dinner catered by the Village's great Italian restaurant Da Silvano. Lots of mouth-watering breads I can't have.

September 27: Ann straps ten pounds on each leg. Heavier weights and fewer repetitions. She is excited about my leg progress and so am I.

September 30: "Your legs are getting there."

October 1: I ask Ann if I can eat a piece of bread. She says I can if I ride an extra fifteen minutes at top speed on the bike. Forget it. She introduces the dreaded purple band—even less resilient than the green.

At dinner that night, I sit next to Dr. Isador Rosenfeld, heart doctor to the stars, who doesn't understand why I can't drink bubbly water or champagne. I don't either, but Ann keeps promising to get me the answer.

October 2: Today Ann has a one-inch circular blue band waiting for me. She likes to find new "apparatuses" to vary my workout. She teaches me a long and repetitive routine using the blue band.

Over the weekend I faithfully do my new exercises plus my old ones—well over an hour's worth every day. On Saturday night I cheat on my diet with something profoundly vulgar—the chocolate frosting and the white squiggle on top of a "light" Hostess Cupcake. I haven't had a Hostess Cupcake since I was a kid. My sister never touched one. Come to think of it, not a drop of carbonated anything has ever passed my sister's lips either.

October 7: I ask Ann about measuring my thighs. "I don't like measuring and weighing and counting calories. I like it for you and me to notice a difference in this room." I measure myself at home and find I've lost an inch on each thigh.

I bike every day, usually for thirty-four minutes at level four. (To heck with fifty-two minutes at level two.) They both burn off about the same number of calories, but Ann prefers the longer ride. I hate it. It's boring and almost impossible to read because the bike is in the massage room—a dark room with gray walls and a low-watt bulb in the ceiling. Nevertheless, I have logged quite a few books on the bike. Right now I'm deep into *Oblomov* by Ivan Goncharov. Oblomov rarely rises before four in the afternoon and wouldn't dream of dressing without the help of his servant. He makes sloth sound noble.

October 15: I bike for fifty-two minutes to the pages of *Oblomov.* I come home exhausted, slip into a hot tub with bubbles, and decide to have steak tonight—a no-no. The phone rings. "I'm calling to invite you to a free workout at the Excelsior Athletic Club. Are you interested?" Ha!

October 31 (Halloween): I eat ten corn candies. "If you were going to cheat, you should have done something better than that," says Ann. "I like the way your legs are looking, though. They're slimming well on the lower thigh." Today she focuses on my adductors, where the cellulite is. "This is what we're going to be working on now. So you really have to be extra good about what you eat." How can I be any better? Everybody is telling me I look too thin. What I'm learning, though, is that exercise can be addictive. You get hooked by the process and keep seeing light at the end of the tunnel. A mirage?

November 11: Ann is disappointed in my adductors. "Too much cellulite. More than when we started." Merciful heavens! Is that possible? "I think it's just that the leg is changing. I can see a thin leg underneath it."

November 20: Ann asks me if I could work with her for an extra month—through January. "Sometimes when a body goes through all this, it reaches a plateau. Your legs look good, but I want to take them to that next step."

November 22: It's Ann's birthday and we celebrate with bubbles—my first Pellegrino.

November 23: "Your legs look better. But now I'm going to have to take your butt down to match your legs." She gives me a pair of two-pound weights to take home, and a week's worth of exercises to do while I'm away for the Thanksgiving holiday. I do my exercises dutifully. There's a list of yeses and nos for Thanksgiving day. The last one, a yes, reads, "One forkful of pumpkin pie!"

Since *Oblomov,* I've read *Brideshead Revisited, A Room With a View,* and Sybille Bedford's *Jigsaw: An Unsentimental Education.* Seems as though I favor the Brits for bike-time reading.

December 9: Ann introduces me to the Thigh Master and gives me one to take home. When I walk in the front door, my husband asks, "What's that?" and then tries to use it himself. It's a blue-and-red plastic spring mechanism that's supposed to make your legs look like those of Suzanne Somers, who is stretched out in a lissome, leggy pose on the box it comes in.

December 10: "I'd like to get some more off around the outer thigh, lift your butt and make it smaller." We add step exercises to the bike routine—and of course, continue my Thigh Mastering every day at home.

Ann says I can relax the diet for Christmas. I have my first Diet Coke since July 27. Heaven! Then I hit the bike.

January 3: I'm still riding the damn bike every day.

January 8: "I really see a difference. The

whole leg has come down, but you've still got to ride." I do so assiduously for the rest of the month, under Ann's watchful eye.

January 24: At last! Ann says she has the answer to the bubble mystery. According to her Diet guru, carbonated drinks (1) have a lot of carbon dioxide, which causes bloating; (2) are high in sodium, which is water-retentive; (3) contain caffeine, which is an appetite stimulant.

Okay. But wait a minute. Carbonated Poland Spring water is "naturally sodium-free," and the diet Coke I used to drink is caffeine-free. When I point this out to Ann, she reluctantly okays my Poland Spring water. But when I get home, I find a message from her: "Don't drink *any* bubbles."

The next day, she hands me a note from her "applied kinesiologist": "The carbonated water (bubbles) causes an acidic environment," it reads, "which makes digestion harder. The body retains water in order to dilute the acidity and aid in the digestion."

After six months of waiting for the word on bubbles, I'm just not convinced. I make some calls and am led to Dr. Jack Wilmore, a professor of kinesiology at the University of Texas at Austin. He listens to my tale and bursts out laughing. "That's great," he says. "I love it. I'm just getting ready to speak on crazy diets, and this takes the cake. I'd like to see some evidence—where's the research that supports it?" I can't bring myself to tell him that I'm it.

My ordeal with a personal trainer is over. I'm in self-regulated "maintenance"—an hour a day of stepping and weights at home; bread (without butter) occasionally; and a bubble drink whenever

I want it (don't tell Ann). I've lost two inches from the trouble area of my upper thighs, and the rest of the leg is thinner and more clearly defined. Ann Piccirillo has all her trainees on bubble-free diets now, on the strength of her success with me.

The bottom line is I like the way my new legs look and feel. My jeans are baggy. My cellulite is in remission. But let's face it, I'm never going to be Suzanne Somers. And unless I keep up a strict regime of diet and exercise for the rest of time, I'll be right back where I started. Ann worked me harder than I would ever have worked on my own or in a class, and she has given me the motivation to keep going—at least I hope she has.

If skirt lengths really come down again, though, I might just find myself a kinesiologist (whatever that means) who'll let me eat Hostess cupcakes.

July 1992

hemlines

It's spring—and I'm in a dither about hemlines. I know this marks me as a quivering fashion victim, but I can't help it. Karl Lagerfeld says skirts that are too short look middle-aged—and I hear that Blaine Trump is getting rid of all hers. Geoffrey Beene, *au contraire*, is sticking to his short-skirted, body-revealing, leggy look. The other designers' hemlines are all over the place—short and tight; short and full; long and split; wrapped, long, and fringed; medium and split, front and back, et cetera. And the worst of it is, I need new clothes.

Where to start? I haven't been to the new Galeries Lafayette on Fifty-seventh Street, France's latest export, so I begin there, thinking maybe they can tell me what to do. It doesn't look very Parisian; in fact, it looks a lot like the old Bonwit's, which occupied the premises for umpty-ump years. Jill Page, the head of personal shopping, who's wearing a red dress that ends at midthigh, takes me in hand. "I just went to a Carrie Donovan seminar on this very subject," she tells me when I broach the skirt-length problem. "Carrie says skirts are up and down but that they *are* getting longer."

Jill takes me on a whirlwind tour of the store. She shows me dresses by Courrèges (to the knee), pants by Emmanuelle Khanh, short frocks by Thierry Mugler and Chloé, and many, many pleated skirts by a host of French designers I've never heard of, ranging in length from the knee on up. "Isn't it fun to be a girl?" Jill chirps, holding up a frilly black evening dress that exposes more bosom than leg. "And by the way, you must come to our La Perla bathing-suit show in two weeks." Bathing suits are another problem, one that I don't have to think about right now, thank God. My time is up. I hurry on to my next appointment, more confused than ever.

My next appointment is with Norma Kamali, in her many-leveled boutique a block away. An attractive woman with long, lustrous dark hair and a friendly smile, Norma is wearing one of her own oversize red plaid pantsuits with suede platform sandals. She's only a little taller than I am. "It's not just a question of skirt lengths," she tells me. "I think the world is a very different place, and women can't even consider being dictated to now. Most women. They need guidance and they like to know what's around, but nobody's going to let herself look like a fool anymore."

Since pro-choice is in, Kamali is designing skirts in three lengths: sixteen inches, twenty inches, and thirty-four inches. "So, depending on where you're going, what you're doing, what your legs look like, you certainly should be able to make a decision."

Decisions, though, are what give me the fantods. She tells me to stand up, and I do so, in my one-and-only, just-above-the-knee-length Chanel suit. "That's just right," she says. "Absolutely. You can wear a longer skirt, but I think the twenty-inch length is right for you." Norma Kamali suspects that a lot of women may put aside the short skirt for a while, but not for long. "I think it's still viable," she says. "And whoever has a big wardrobe of short skirts is going to continue wearing them. People don't want disposable clothes now. We're not going to do that to you anymore. You can't afford it, we can't afford it. The extravagance we went through in the eighties was awful. Everybody's got these clothes in their closets from the eighties that they'll never wear, and we can't make clothes like that anymore—we have to be more responsible."

We go one flight down so I can try on a long-sleeved khaki shirtdress with a twenty-inch skirt that she thinks would look "absolutely great" on me. She rolls up the sleeves, opens the neck, and claps on a cinch belt. She's right, I love it. The skirt falls just above my knee. It moves wonderfully. I feel comfortable, and it's only $125. I grab it and run.

"I will not take part in the discussion of longer skirts," intones Geoffrey Beene, the high priest of minimalist couture. "It is not a valid conversation. I have made my decision, and it is up to the customer to make hers."

Beene's decision is to go right on designing the short skirts and body-revealing clothes that have distinguished his line for the last ten years. He's not even recommending the option of pants, which he considers "a cop-out." Sitting in his black-and-silver office, behind his shiny black desk, he tells me about a conversation he had with a flight attendant last Christmas en route to Honolulu. "She came up to me and said, 'Oh, Mr. Beene, I'm so glad you're on the plane, you can help me.' I said, 'In what way?' And she said, 'About hemlines—what length should I wear?' 'How could you possibly ask me that?' I said. 'It's against the whole women's movement.' She replied, 'I was never a part of that.'"

Women have to decide for themselves, in other words, but Geoffrey Beene is not going to give them much choice. "I will not be changing hemlines," he says, "for the simple reason that short dresses let people move more easily. And in a mobile society, in a fast-moving world, it's illogical to do anything that would hinder movement. Modern to me means less fabric. I'm simply saying I prefer to stay modern."

Feeling slightly dictated to about not being dictated to, I leave without trying on anything.

Two days later Michael Kors is telling me that the first question he hears from women around the country is "What's the length?" According to Kors, who looks younger than ever in blue jeans and sneakers, what's happening now is that women's wardrobes are opening up to include a little of everything. "The whole direction now is to realize that women in the nineties have a lot of different moods. Whether you want to feel androgynous and sort of rangy in a trouser and a shirt, or very, very romantic in a soft, full skirt at night, or powerful and provocative in a slit, narrow, long skirt during the day, or if you just want to fall back on the short, narrow skirt that you've lived in, you can do it."

He shows me some flowing, ankle-length slit skirts from his spring collection, but we agree that they're not for me. "Too much skirt for you," he says. "You'd look like you were in an evening gown. A short woman can wear a long skirt, but you need to see her legs. Proportion is what counts. But we're going into a whole cycle of fashion change now, and it's not a question of some designer saying 'Let there be long.' Short is not disappearing. We're still doing short skirts but with some movement to them. Wrapped, slit, maybe cut on the bias, softer. It's about pretty. It's not about *La Femme Nikita*, I'm-going-to-hit-you-over-the-head, I'm-powerful kind of look."

I try on a few things. What looks best is a pleated black knit skirt that's flat through the hips, with a lot of bouncy movement at the bottom. It's about two inches shorter than my usual length, but I like it. It doesn't make me look like a cheerleader or a carhop. "I think it's fine short," he says. "You look nineties." It's the perfect skirt, it costs $250, and I take it in two shades—black and toast.

At Martha, where "Miss Lynn," the founder's daughter, continues the tradition of highly personalized service, I step into a powder pink world of mirrors, chandeliers, and chintz. Miss Lynn, who reminds me a little of Eva Gabor, is just my size. "Because of my own stature, I can relate to you instantaneously," she says, beaming. She sits me down on a sofa and ushers in a model (not my stature, as usual) wearing Karl Lagerfeld's double-barreled cocktail suit—a below-the-calf black chiffon skirt with a black microskirt showing through underneath. "I think this is the real news right here," she says. "We're not imposing just one length. We're telling a girl she can have both, which is a wonderful way to go. I'm crazy about Karl's sultry, sassy look, and I think we're going to sell it very well."

The model goes away and comes back in a Bill Blass suit with a long, narrow slit skirt. "Bill told me that he didn't want to impose," says Miss Lynn, "so he's come out with two versions." The other one is a short skirt. "But it's funny, with the short skirt it looks like something you've had."

Now it's a three-piece outfit by Andrea Jovine—a form-fitting black wool jersey skirt that ends between ankle and calf, with a rump-high slit up the back; black vest to match; voluptuously scaled white blouse. "You can start at eight in the morning like that and be perfect at midnight," Miss Lynn says. Maybe, although not in my line of work. I try it on anyway. Not bad. The whole outfit costs $750. I'll think about it.

I'm way downtown today at Isaac Mizrahi's loft showroom in SoHo. Isaac, who has just turned thirty, is wearing a black piqué collarless suit he designed for himself, and black Hush Puppies. He's a wonderful talker—being with Isaac is better than most movies, and certainly better than going to your shrink.

"It's the end of fashion tyranny, don't you think?" he asks. "Unless you're talking about those reactionaries in Paris. What was that silly quote of Karl Lagerfeld's? He said short skirts look middle-aged. I say anything is possible."

One thing he doesn't think is possible, though, is the short-short skirt. "Things have changed so much socially and politically and economically," he says. "It's really nasty to show your legs like that, to be that obvious and that vulgar. Five years ago, I was all about color and very short skirts and the glorification of the female form in its most uncovered state. But now I feel that there are ways of being exuberant, jaunty, happy—all those things we want to be—and discreet at the same time. That trashy ideal of beauty for the past seven years—big blond hair and big boobs and tight, tight clothes—I've been moving away from that. I really feel as though clothes have to whisper and not be the primary point of reference."

He's been doing longer skirts for a couple of years now, and he says his fall line "is going to be primarily a longer length for me." There will be some short skirts, but the majority will be mid- to low-calf.

What about me, right now? "You know what?" he says, taking in my black piqué shift that just covers my knee. "This is too long for a short dress, and it should be narrower at the bottom." We go to a large, mirrored room where he's pulled out some clothes for me to try on, including a short hopsack skirt in a color he calls unripe banana. "This would be great on you. See how narrow it is at the bottom? It's perfect right *there*," he says, holding it so it falls just above my knee.

He pulls out a black, strapless, mid-calf-length dress.

"I can wear this?"

"For sure. With a sheer dark leg or a bare leg. My God, it's really good. It makes you taller. A long skirt makes you look really tall. No platform shoes." (Lagerfeld is big on platforms this year.)

"That would ruin it, make it look like fashion. And I can't stand fashion. Who needs fashion today? Fashion is totally out."

I'm almost convinced by the black strapless, but the trouble is, I'm looking for daytime clothes. What I try on instead, and eventually buy for $495, is a blue-and-white-striped shirtdress, just above the knee. Apparently I'm not going to go for a long skirt this time around.

Maybe I'm just chicken. Maybe I'll pull a cop-out and buy myself some new jeans—and a La Perla bathing suit. It's clear that freedom of choice is the wave of the future, but I need more practice. It was so much easier when we were being told what to do—even if we knew we looked ridiculous, at least we had the security of knowing we were *in style*.

Next time, I'll drum up the right pioneer spirit. "We Americans are pioneers," Isaac Mizrahi told me. "Still. And now we have to take a few passionate backward steps, like tango dancers. They step backward passionately and forward passionately. It doesn't matter which way they step. It's always dramatic. I think that the trend into the next century is going to be longer skirts. Skirts are either going to be long or they're not going to exist anymore."

"What will we wear then?" I asked him.

"Bodysuits. No skirts. What a great idea! No skirts—except on men."

May 1992

the little black dress

At least once a year, I have a craving for a new little black dress. Last year, I ignored my craving because I hate to shop, so this year I'm doubly hungry.

My life depends on the little black dress. Wearing one can sometimes make me feel like Audrey Hepburn—who can forget her as Holly Golightly in *Breakfast at Tiffany's*, in that glorious Givenchy that flounced out at the bottom? But it was Chanel who started the whole thing back in 1926. *Vogue* illustrated Chanel's simple black crepe de chine sheath with long, close-fitting sleeves and a knee-high skirt and predicted it would become "a sort of uniform for all women of taste." The copy read, "Here is a Ford, signed 'Chanel.' "

As you can imagine, today there is a little black dress by every designer you've ever heard of, and many more by those you've never heard of. Having decided to limit my search to American designers this time around, I picked out three, and *Vogue* suggested three others.

My first stop is Isaac Mizrahi's in SoHo. The floors are shiny white poured vinyl. A model walks by in a black Mizrahi halfway up her thigh, and Nina Santisi, Mizrahi's right-hand person, calls out, "That skirt is too long. It's dowdy." Feeling dowdy all of a sudden in my just-above-the-knee dress, I'm escorted into a *grande luxe* dressing room, and in comes Isaac.

"Sorry I'm late," he says, all boyish sincerity and hair mousse.

"Who did your suit?" I ask about his blue-gray, almost mauve suit.

"Isaac Mizrahi did," he says. "It's like the color of Elsie de Wolfe's hair. It's good, isn't it?"

We settle down and discuss the life and times of the little black dress. "I think it started when Eve was looking around for a perfect black fig-leaf," he says. "But when I think of the little black dress, I think of Norell, who glorified it. I mean, that was what his whole career was about. I also think about Audrey Hepburn in *Breakfast at Tiffany's*, living every single day in the same black dress with different accessories and making it look new every day. And I think about a woman in the nineties who needs to wear the same thing from eight in the morning until midnight."

Can anybody wear a little black dress?

"Anybody. Any age. For sure. I have a few in mind for you," he tells me. He shows me a black wool jersey with a big taffeta ruffle around the off-the-shoulder neckline. Also a turtleneck knit with taffeta-ruffled shoulders. (Both cost about $750.) Then there's a perfectly simple black stretch crepe that zips up the front and has a deep V neck. "It goes anywhere," he says about this one, which is as décolleté as the law allows. "It could go black-tie, for sure, with the right diamond choker. Or you can put a giant scarf in the bust and have it look appropriate for the office."

Now he's holding up a black suede shift with fringe just under the bust. Next a bare satin-topped, ballerina-type dress. Then a simple black dress that has "the propriety of a sweater set and the shape of a serpent." Then one with ostrich-feathered arms.

Enough. One is more fantastical than the next. I'd like to try the off-the-shoulder with the taffeta ruffle, but it's market week, and too many potential store buyers are focused on it. So I start with the ballerina dress. It buckles like a belt, but of course it's too big. It's the old problem—I'm five feet two and long to be five six. To make things worse, it's the week after the fall collections, so everything I try on is cut for a six-foot model.

"It should be a little shorter, for sure. And not quite as excessive in the skirt," Isaac says. He also tells me that I should wear more makeup. (They all do.)

I'm actually looking for a black dress that is less attention-getting, so I get into the jersey turtleneck with taffeta ruffles on the shoulders. Even two sizes too large, it's too short for me.

"It's not too short for you," says Isaac. "As a matter of fact, I think it could be a little bit shorter with opaque black hose. In other words, if your leg were more opaque, you'd want your skirt right there," he says, hiking up the already too-short dress another two inches. "And suddenly your legs would be completely long."

But aren't my legs too fat?

"When you walk into a room, women might say, 'Oh, look at those fat legs.' But all the men love legs like yours. Now, *I* have fat legs," he says, lifting his trouser to make me feel better.

I feel a little better, but I have to leave without trying on the off-the-shoulder big-taffeta-ruffle job.

I'm on Seventh Avenue now, in Donna Karan's office. It's black tables, white walls, mirrors, racks of clothes, peonies, and platters of fruit. Donna is late. I start my striptease to get into a black merino wool dress with a pleated skirt. It looks great. Then I get into one that is like a bodysuit with a sarong attached. Very sophisticated.

"Oh, you're already dressed!" It's Donna. She's much taller than I expect, wearing black, black, black. "The first thing I'd do is darken your legs," she says. "The success of black is that you have a oneness from head to toe. So I try to matte everything out. Matte the shoe. Matte the leg. Then you don't have to worry about 'Are my legs great or not?' What *you* want to do—because of your height—is keep the line as unbroken as possible. Basically, you wear petite."

I hate the word *petite*. It makes me feel shrimplike.

"Can we put the opaque legs on her?"

Patti Cohen, Donna's chief PR and advertising honchesse, hands me a pair of black jersey hose by Donna. All she can find is extra long. Donna tells Patti she'd like to put me into "the little matte jersey with the circular skirt."

"We don't have it," Patti says.

Donna seems not to have heard her. "That's going to be the number-one-selling dress. But you know which one everybody loves? The Lycra scoop-neck top with the wool ottoman skirt. It's the basic black dress."

Neither dress comes on command. But she's focused on my legs now. "Do you feel the difference the minute you put on the matte hose? You don't see where your leg begins or ends, nor where the skirt begins or ends. This skirt should be shorter. The whole concept of the way I design is as if you're wearing a black leotard."

I'm still in the sarong bodydress, and she's on the floor tightening my bodysuit at the crotch with safety pins. "Does it feel better?"

"I guess," I answer. Except that I'm afraid to move, for fear of being stabbed.

"Do you feel like a different person?"

I do. I do. And I like the price—$600. I would still like to try on the Lycra-and-ottoman that she predicts will be the basic black dress this year. But it never materializes, and I'm getting late for my appointment with Geoffrey Beene.

"I'm saying this is the perfect little black dress if you have a perfect figure," says Geoffrey Beene. We're in his opulently sparse office with silver-leaf walls. The dress he's talking about is on a mannequin. No more than a yard of fabric in all, it costs $2,400 and exposes a wide swath of female anatomy winding from shoulder to buttocks to thigh, under a film of point d'esprit lace. "It's my favorite," he says, with a slight drawl that hints at his Louisiana roots. "It's the most demanding of the figure. It suggests, but it reveals nothing. It's exploring the body but not exploiting it. I studied medicine—four years—so I know and respect the body. The dress does not even have a zipper in it because the zipper would weigh more than the dress."

"What do you wear under this dress?" I ask him.

"The perfect body. That's all. And shoes, to keep your feet clean. It requires courage and confidence. I don't design for women who are not confident and courageous."

Would this dress work for me?

"Oh, for you," he says, rather haughtily. "I would not suggest that this is the perfect dress for you. It's the perfect dress for me to design."

He whips out a tiny pad of paper and sketches a dress from the collection that he says will be perfect for me. It's a black double-faced crepe long-sleever with an industrial zipper in front from neck to hem. No body exploration here, I can see. And not much confidence or courage required, either. Forget it.

My pride gets the better of me, and I try on the $2,400 body revealer. It goes on all right, but too much of me is out there on view. The peekaboo-lace panel is too much peek and not enough boo. I don't show it to Geoffrey Beene.

"I don't know if I design the perfect black dress for everyone," he tells me. "I'm not sure I would wish to. Black dresses are very special. In no way are they basic here. A basic dress implies a dumb dress."

Chastened and a little crestfallen, I slink away and head for Badgley Mischka, where it feels more like SoHo than Seventh Avenue. I find James Mischka and Mark Badgley in a sea of little black dresses. It seems this is a specialty of these rising stars. "It's what we do," says Mark, the one with dark hair.

"We keep reperfecting it," says James. He and Mark, who are both thirty, went into business together two years ago. They say their little black dresses were inspired by Audrey Hepburn in *Breakfast at Tiffany's* (as does almost everyone I see) but also by John Singer Sargent's famous portrait of Madame X. I see so many little black dresses that I don't know where to start. There are a lot of décolleté necklines, most are ornamented with lace or jet beading, and many have names. "All our cocktail dresses have cocktail names," says James.

Badgley and Mischka don't believe in the concept of day-into-evening dressing. "We love the idea of a girl going home, taking her bath, and putting something dressy on at night," says Mark.

They decide what I should try on, thank God. Over the next half hour, I'm in and out of the Tom Collins, the Reno, the Delmonico, and the Bacardi. Also the Jezebel, a real man-getter—V neck, fitted bodice, flared skirt—which Mark says overpowers me. After these, I try on an unnamed, simple, classically cut dress made of baby bouclé that skims my tiring body. (It's $970, including a little black jacket.) It feels wonderfully soothing, like my one and only Chanel suit. I'm drunk with little black dresses. How will I ever decide?

I take the weekend to recuperate, but Monday morning I'm at it again. This time it's Michael Kors. Right off he shows me the black lace dress that he describes as "sort of right now." It's narrow through the waist and fitted on the top of the hip, and there's movement at the bottom. "It's a very different feeling from the black dresses that people wore in the eighties, which were all about body, narrow hem, tortured fit, tart, tart, tart," he says. "Now it's a lot softer. It's comfortable and very feminine."

Is the little black dress a New York and Paris phenomenon, I ask, or is it more universal now?

"For years everyone thought it was very New York. Now it's very L.A. California is feeling very urban, and I think the black dress connotes urban. It's all about chic. It's sophisticated and versatile. Women *collect* little black dresses. If you have a lot in your closet already, the new one really has to seduce you."

We go into his black-and-white (workmanlike chic) office so I can be seduced. When I hesitate to undress in front of him, he throws up his hands. "Oh, Gaad," he moans. "Most New Yorkers will get undressed in the middle of Times Square. In London they'll have a nervous breakdown—'Don't come in.' And in Los Angeles they'll show you their latest surgery."

He wants me to try on the A-line lace "dress of the season," which I do, as soon as he absents himself. It's a great fit, not too short, with a scoop neck and a flared skirt (something Donna Karan told me I should avoid). "It's adorable on you," he says, coming back into the room. "I'd just take a little off the cap sleeves."

Is it okay for me to expose so much arm?

"It's okay for you," he says. "You don't have UADD—that's Under Arm Dingle Dangle."

I'm charmed but not quite seduced. Onward!

It's Bill Blass week at Martha's. Posters in the window promise he'll be there to show his collection to the Faithful—the devoted Blass ladies who make him the reigning monarch of American fashion. Handsome, faultlessly dressed, he comes in from lunch at 3:00 P.M. and, though we've never met, greets me like an old friend.

"The little black dress has never been stronger than it is right at this moment," he says. "Do you have that feeling, too? It is literally *the* uniform again. Psychologically, the black dress makes you look thinner and smaller if you're big, and it makes you feel more important if you're small. Isn't that funny?"

Contessa Something or Other, wearing a T-shirt that says DARE TO BE SEXY, swoops down to press Bill's hand in both of hers. He responds with practiced charm. When he gets his hand back, he tells me that the black dresses that first inspired him were Norman Norell's. "He was always the one I looked up to the most. He was from Indiana, like me, and I followed his career from the time I was a kid. He was a perfectionist at cutting clothes. The black dress depends heavily on the proper cut.

"Do you wear black dresses a lot?" he asks. "You do? Stand up a second. What size are you? Two? I think you need long sleeves. You need more dress, since there's very little of you."

He knows exactly the dress for me, and he goes off to fetch it. "This is my favorite," he says, holding up a long-sleeved, high-necked satin-back crepe that is definitely important. Several ladies, overhearing him, clearly resent my temporary possession of it. It looks very elegant on me, very grown-up. Maybe a little too grown-up. I take it off, and Bill Blass immediately commandeers it for one of the Faithful.

Decision time. I've spent a week and a half looking at little black dresses, and I'm the victim of too much good advice. Donna Karan and Isaac Mizrahi like short, short skirts with opaque black legs; Michael Kors favors more length and less opacity. I've heard a lot about black dresses so versatile that they will take you through the day and into the evening, but Bill Blass and Badgley Mischka consider that infra dig. And I agree. Who wants to wear the same dress for twelve hours straight? My courage and confidence, my femininity, my height, and my legs have been put to the test, all for a wisp of black cloth.

I wish I had been able to try on Donna Karan's Lycra-and-ottoman "basic black dress" and Isaac Mizrahi's number with the ruffle around the top (for sure). But, more and more, I keep thinking about Badgley Mischka's baby bouclé classic. It felt new without straining for newness, and I felt like me in it. After all the looking and talking and theorizing, my decision is absurdly subjective. I'll take the Badgley Mischka. For me, it's right because it's right.

July 1991